The Norse Gods

An Illustrated Introduction

Matthew Leigh Embleton

Copyright ©2024 Matthew Leigh Embleton. All rights reserved.

The Norse Gods

Introduction 5
01 The Æsir 1
   Almáttki Áss (Unnamed God of Oaths) 1
   Baldr (God of Light, Joy, Purity, Peace, and Forgiveness) 2
   Bragi (God of Poetry, Speech, and Music) 4
   Dellingr (God of Light and the Dawn) 6
   Forseti (God of Justice and Reconciliation) 7
   Heimdall (God of Light, Watchman of the Gods) 9
   Hermodr (The Messenger of the Gods) 11
   Hodr (God of Winter, Cold, and Darkness) 13
   Hoenir (God of Silence and Spirituality) 15
   Lodurr (Creator of Humans) 17
   Loki (God of Trickery) 18
   Mani (God of the Moon) 20
   Mimir (God of Wisdom) 21
   Modi and Magni (The Wrathful and Mighty Sons of Thor) 22
   Odin (The Allfather) 23
   Odr (The Absent Wanderer and God of Passion or Frenzy) 25
   Thor (God of Thunder and Lightning) 26
   Tyr (God of War, Warriors, Law, and Justice) 28
   Ullr (God of Winter and Skiing) 30
   Vali (The Divine Avenger) 32
   Vidarr (The Silent Avenger) 34
   Vili and Ve (Brothers of Odin) 36
02 The Ásynjur 37
   Bil and Hjuki (The Followers of the Moon) 37
   Eir (Goddess of Healing, the Healing Arts, and Medical Skill) 38
   Frigg (Goddess of Marriage, Prophecy, and Motherhood) 40
   Fulla (Goddess of Plenty, Wealth, and Abundance) 42
   Gefjon (Goddess of Ploughing, Foreknowledge, and Chastity) 43
   Gerdr (Goddess of the Earth) 45
   Gna and Hofvarpnir (Messengers of Frigg) 47
   Hlin (The Protector and Giver of Refuge) 48
   Idunn (Goddess of Apples and Eternal Youth) 49
   Lofn (Goddess of Marriage and Union) 51
   Nanna (Wife of Baldr) 52
   Njorun (Mysterious Goddess of the Earth) 53
   Ran (Goddess of the Sea) 54
   Rindr (Mother of Vali, The Divine Avenger) 56
   Saga (The Seeress) 57
   Sif (Goddess of Fertility, Family, and Wedlock) 58
   Sigyn (Wife of Loki) 60
   Sjofn (Goddess of Love) 61
   Skadi (Goddess of Winter and Mountains) 62
   Snotra (Goddess of Wisdom) 64
   Sol (Goddess of the Sun) 65
   Syn (Goddess of Defence and Refusal) 66
   Var (Goddess of Oaths and Agreements) 67
   Vor (Goddess of Wisdom) 68
03 The Vanir 69

    Freyja (Goddess of Love, Beauty, Fertility, War, Gold, and Magic) 69
    Freyr (God of Kingship, Fertility, Prosperity, and Peace) 71
    Gullveig (The Golden Sorceress) 73
    Kvasir (Poet, Scholar, and Wisest of All) 74
    Njord (God of the Sea) 75
04 The Jotnar (Giants) 77
05 The Dvergar (Dwarves) 85
06 Others 88
    Fenrir: The Giant Wolf 88
    Hel: Keeper of the Underworld 90
    Jormungandr: The World Serpent 92
    The Nornir: The Three Fates 94
    Yggdrasil: The World Tree 96
07 Interesting Objects 98

Cover: A Norse Temple
Source: AI Generated by the author

Acknowledgments

I have long been fascinated by languages and history, and I am very grateful to the special people in my life who have supported and encouraged me in my work. Thank you for believing in me. You know who you are.

Introduction

The Norse gods are the key players in Norse mythology, an ancient collection of narratives that evolved over centuries to explain the origins of the forces of nature around us, their impact on our lives, the nature of humankind itself, what it means to be human, our relationship with the earth and the cosmos, and our sense of place within it.

There are a number of similarities between Norse mythology and Greco-Roman mythology in terms of creation and cosmology, human-god relationships, heroic myths, the afterlife, and the concept of fate. The Norse gods possess supernatural powers and control various aspects of the natural world. They are divided into two main groups, the *Æsir* and the *Vanir*. The *Æsir*, led by Odin, are associated with war and wisdom (the female deities in this group are collectively called the *Ásynjur*). The *Vanir*, led by Njord, are associated with fertility and prosperity.

The conflict between the *Æsir* and the *Vanir* is known as the *Æsir-Vanir* War, which ultimately results in their unification into a single pantheon. This war is seen as a reflection of the struggles between various Germanic and Indo-European peoples across Europe from as early as 1000 BCE until the Migration Period around the decline and fall of the Western Roman Empire (300-600 CE). This was a struggle between fertility cults and aggressive warlike cults, land and territory, religion and worship. As the people battled over territory and whose gods held sway, the gods battled between themselves over the souls of those who worshipped them.

Part of what we know about Norse mythology and the wider Germanic mythology is from the writings of those who encountered those who believed in it. Roman historian Tacitus in his first century work known as *Germania*, saw parallels from his Roman perspective between Odin and Mercury (rather than Zeus or Jupiter), and between Thor and Hercules.

Another part of what we know about Norse mythology comes from Old Norse inscriptions, and also texts, the majority of which were created in Iceland, where the oral tradition of the pre-Christian inhabitants was collected and recorded in manuscripts. This process took place in the 12th and 13th centuries. This includes works such as Saxo Grammaticus's *Gesta Danorum* (The Deeds of the Danes), the *Poetic Edda*, a collection of poems from traditional material compiled anonymously, the *Prose Edda*, written and compiled in the 13th century by Icelandic historian Snorri Sturluson, and also the many sagas and tales.

When reading the names and the texts of the original Old Norse, it is worth familiarising oneself with two extra letters: Thorn = Þ, þ which represents the unvoiced 'th' sound as in 'think', and 'thought', 'through' later replaced by 'th'. Eth = Ð, ð which represents the voiced 'th' sound as in 'the', 'this', and 'that', later replaced by 'th' or 'd'. These letters were used in Old English a thousand years ago but began to fall out of use after 1066. However, they are still used in modern Icelandic.

Several gods and goddesses in the Norse pantheon are believed to have been different versions of each other, worshipped in different areas, at different times, with different names, but with similarities in the details of their stories and legends. There were hundreds years of oral tradition and storytelling all over Northern Europe before the events and relationships between the gods started to be written down.

What sets Norse mythology uniquely apart from others is the emphasis on courage, honour, loyalty, and the warrior code. The Norse gods focus more on natural phenomena and war. They are more human-like with their flaws, emotions, and mortality. The structure of their stories is less clearly defined with more overlapping contradictions. The Norse gods and their mythology have influenced art, literature, and popular culture for centuries, and continue to do so today.

01 The Æsir

Almáttki Áss (Unnamed God of Oaths)

Almáttki Áss is an unknown Norse god evoked in an Icelandic legal oath sworn on a temple ring described in *Landnámabók* ('the book of land-takers' or 'settlers'). The unnamed god was important enough to witness sworn oaths, and to be written about, even if their real identity or any other information about them is now lost to us.

Rings have a very prominent position in early Germanic cultures. They appear throughout areas settled by Germanic peoples, and in textual sources discussing their practices and beliefs. As well as their association with swearing oaths witnessed by gods, they are also associated with aspects of wealth and gift-giving, and used in forms of currency in the Early Medieval Period.

Arm, finger and neck rings dating back to the Early Medieval Period have been found in hoards throughout Northern Europe, such as the Spillings Hoard found on the Swedish island of Gotland in 1999, and the Silverdale Hoard in Lancashire, England found in 2011.

*"Nefni ek í þat vætti, skyldi hann segja, "at ek vinn eið at baugi, lögeið. Hjálpi mér svá Freyr ok Njörðr ok inn **almáttki Áss** sem ek mun svá sök þessa sækja eða verja eða vitni bera eða kviðu eða dæma sem ek veit réttast ok sannast ok helzt at lögum ok öll lögmæt skil af hendi leysa, þau er undir mik koma, meðan ek em á þessu þingi."*

"Name I to witness", should he say, "that I take an oath on the ring, lawfully. Help me so Freyr and Njord and the **almighty god** as I so seek this case and defend or testify bear and forebode or deem as I know is right and true and most to law and all lawfully return of hand solution, that which under me comes, while I am at this assembly."

Halsring neck ring, the Vandalic Treasure of Osztrópataka
Kunsthistorisches Museum in Vienna, Austria
Creative Commons, Public Domain

Baldr (God of Light, Joy, Purity, Peace, and Forgiveness)

Baldr (Balder, Baldur) is a member of the *Æsir*. The many variations of his name come from the Proto-Germanic *'*Balðraz'*, all giving meanings such as 'bold', 'brave', 'confident', 'courageous', 'defiant', 'frank', 'great man', 'hard', 'hero', 'lord', 'prince', 'stubborn', and 'valiant'.

Baldr is the son of Odin and Frigg, and the brother of Bragi, Heimdall, Hermodr, Hodr, Thor, Tyr, Vali, and Vidarr. He is also the husband of Nanna, and the father of Forseti.

He is described as handsome with the fairest of features, the wisest and fairest-spoken of the *Æsir*, with a bright light that shines from him.

Baldr's ship is called *Hringhorni* ('ring-horn'), which is said to be the largest ship ever built. His dwelling place is called *Breiðablik* ('broad-shining') and is described as a beautiful and heavenly place where nothing unclean may be.

In the *Poetic Edda*, Baldr's death is foretold in *Völuspá* ('The Prophecy of the Völva').

31. *"Ek sá Baldri, blóðgum tívur,*
Óðins barni, örlög folgin;
stóð of vaxinn völlum hæri
mjór ok mjök fagr mistilteinn."

"I saw Baldr, the bleeding god,
Odin's son, destiny followed;
stood of grown fields high
slender and much fair mistletoe."

32. *"Varð af þeim meiði, er mær sýndisk,*
harmflaug hættlig, Höðr nam skjóta;
Baldrs bróðir var of borinn snemma,
sá nam Óðins sonr einnættr vega."

"Became of that hurt, which slender seemed
a dangerous shaft, that Hodr shot;
Baldr's brother was born early,
So took Odin's son one night to slay."

In the poem *Baldrs Draumar* ('Baldr's Dreams'), also known as *Vegtamskviða* ('The Lay of Vegtam'), Baldr has had a series of nightmares that he will be killed. Taking these dreams seriously as a prophecy, the gods hold a council to discuss Baldr's dreams. Odin then disguises himself as a wanderer named Vegtam and rides to Hel (the underworld). While in Hel, Odin uses magic to awaken a völva (seeress) from her grave to ask her who will kill his son Baldr. Odin is told that it is Hodr who will kill Baldr, and that Vali will avenge his death when he is one night old.

In the *Prose Edda* in *Gylfaginning* ('The Beguiling of Gylfi'), the story of Baldr's death is told in more detail, beginning with Baldr's bad dreams, and the council of the *Æsir* discussing the matter. Then Baldr's mother Frigg, who has also had the same dream of Baldr's death, commands all things across the Nine Realms to promise not to hurt Baldr, but the mistletoe ("a tree-sprout alone westward of Valhalla") does not make the promise. Frigg is unconcerned by this, as she does not believe this is of any importance. The gods then amuse themselves by hurling objects at Baldr and watching them bounce off him, causing him no harm at all. Loki learns of what has happened by disguising himself as a woman and asking Frigg what the *Æsir* are up to at their assembly. He then makes a spear (in some accounts an arrow or dart) out of the mistletoe. Loki then tricks Hodr into throwing the spear (or firing the arrow or dart) of mistletoe and inadvertently killing Baldr, his own brother.

The gods are speechless and devastated by Baldr's death. Beings from all of the Nine Realms attend Baldr's funeral. When Baldr's widow Nanna sees Baldr's corpse being carried to his ship *Hringhorni* to be burnt, she dies from her grief. Upon Frigg's request, Hermodr rides to the realm of Hel and speaks to Hel herself, begging for Baldr's release. Hel says that Baldr will only be released if all things, dead and alive, weep for him. All do except for a giantess named Thokk (believed to be Loki in disguise), and so Baldr has to remain in the underworld. Odin and Rindr (a giantess, goddess, or human princess) give birth to Vali who grows to adulthood in a single day and slays Hodr as punishment for killing his own brother.

In *Lokasenna* ('Loki's Verbal Duel'), Baldr's mother Frigg tells Loki that if she had a son like Baldr with her now, Loki would be killed. Loki replies by cruelly taunting Frigg and reminding her of his responsibility for Baldr's death, and that he is the reason she shall no more see Baldr riding home.

Loki's is later caught and sentenced to be bound and tortured. Skadi is tasked with holding a giant serpent above Loki's head, and venom from the fangs of the giant serpent drips into Loki's eyes, which causes Loki unimaginable pain, and he writhes in agony, causing earthquakes in the process.

Baldr's death is the greatest of tragedies to have ever befallen among gods and men, and the first in a chain of events that ultimately leads to *Ragnarök* ('the Twilight of the Gods'), a foretold series of impending events, including a great battle in which many including the gods will die, a series of catastrophic natural disasters, the burning of the world, and the submersion of the world underwater, after which the world will rise again, cleansed and fertile, being repopulated by the survivors. Stanza 62 of *Völuspá* looks far into the future to a time when Hodr and Baldr will return and dwell in Valhalla:

*"Munu ósánir
akrar vaxa,
böls mun alls batna,
Baldr mun koma;
búa þeir Höðr ok Baldr
Hrofts sigtoftir,
vé valtíva.
Vituð ér enn - eða hvat?"*

"Shall unsown
The fields grow,
Ills will get better,
Baldr will come back;
They will dwell, Hodr and Baldr
In Hropt's (Odin's) hall of victory,
House, gods of the slain.
Will you know yet more, or what?"

Left: An illustration of Baldr's death
SÁM 66, c. 1765-1766
Creative Commons, Public Domain

Bragi (God of Poetry, Speech, and Music)

Bragi is a member of the *Æsir*. He is the master of skaldic poetry. The word skald in Old Norse (*skáld*) translates as 'poet'. Skaldic poetry traditionally relies on alliteration instead of rhyme to drive the rhythm and underlying structure.

The name Bragi probably comes from the Old Norse '*bragr*', and the modern Icelandic '*bragur*', which variously translates as 'poetry', 'poem', 'melody', 'wise', 'wisdom' or 'the first' and 'the noblest'.

Bragi is traditionally depicted with a harp (which in ancient times was often used to accompany poetry).

Bragi is the son of Odin and Frigg, and the brother of Baldr, Heimdall, Hermodr, Hodr, Thor, Tyr, Vali, and Vidarr, and he is the husband of Idunn.

In the *Prose Edda* in *Gylfaginning* ('The Beguiling of Gylfi'), Bragi is described as being renowned for his wisdom, fluency of speech, and skill with words. He is also described as the inventor of poetry, after whom the art of poetry is named.

"Bragi heitir einn. Hann er ágætur að speki og mest að málsnilld og orðfimi.

Hann kann mest af skáldskap, og af honum er bragur kallaður skáldskapur,

og af hans nafni er sá kallaður bragur karla eða kvenna er orðsnilld hefur framar en aðrir, kona eða karlmaður."

"Bragi is named one. He is renowned of wisdom and the most to eloquence and skill in words.

He is the most skilled in the art of poetry, and of him is Bragur called the art of poetry,

and of his name are so called Bragur- -man or -woman who have word-skill above others, women or men."

In the *Prose Edda* in *Skáldskaparmál* ('The Language of Poetry'), Bragi is introduced:

"Hvernig skal kenna Braga? Svá, at kalla hann Iðunnar ver, frumsmið bragar ok inn síðskeggja ás - af hans nafni er sá kallaðr skeggbragi, er mikit skegg hefir - ok sonr Óðins."

"How shall Bragi be described? So, to call him the husband of Idunn, the first maker of poetry and the long-bearded god - of his name are so called Beard-Braggi, who great beards have - and son of Odin."

Also in *Skáldskaparmál*, Bragi and Ægir discuss stories of the *Æsir*, the nature of poetry, and tales of human heroes and kings. This work gradually settles into an instructional manual of poetry intended for the use of skalds. Poetic phrases and descriptions called kennings are discussed at length. For example:

Kenning	Translation:	Meaning:
'blóð-eisu'	'blood-ember'	axe
'spjót-djöfull'	'spear-din'	battle
'bardaga-sviti'	'battle-sweat'	blood
'svarraði-sárgymir'	'wound-sea'	blood
'svefn-sverðsins'	'sleep of the sword'	death
'logandi-kveðja'	'flame-farewelled'	killed
'grand-viðar'	'bane of wood'	fire
'weorð-myndum'	'mind-worthiness'	honour
'fæða-erninn'	'to feed the eagle'	to kill one's enemies
'bann-Baldrs'	'Baldr's bane'	mistletoe
'reord-berend'	'voice-bearer'	person
'blóð-svanur'	'swan of blood'	raven
'hron-rād'	'whale-road'	the sea
'sverða-nesi'	'headland of swords'	shield
'heofon-candel'	'heaven's candle'	the sun
'vopna-veður'	'weather of weapons'	war
'trjá-brjótur'	'breaker of trees'	wind

Idunn and Bragi by Nils Blommér, 1846
Creative Commons, Public Domain

Dellingr (God of Light and the Dawn)

Dellingr is a member of the *Æsir*. He is either the third husband of Nott (the personification of night) or the husband of Jord (the personification of the Earth), depending on manuscript sources.

He is also the father of Dagr (the personification of the day), and scholars suggest that he is the personification of the dawn. His name in Old Norse possibly means 'the dayspring' or 'the shining one'.

In the *Poetic Edda* in *Vafþrúðnismál*, Odin (disguised as Gagnráðr) engages in a battle of wits with Vafþrúðnir. Odin asks where the day comes from, and the night and its tides:

Gagnráðr
"Seg þú þat it þriðja,
alls þik svinnan kveða
ok þú, Vafþrúðnir, vitir,
hvaðan dagr of kom,
sá er ferr drótt yfir,
eða nótt með niðum."

Gagnradr (Odin)
"Say you a third thing,
as you are called wise
and you, Vafthrudnir, know,
from-where does the day come,
so travels drawn over,
and night among goes down."

Vafþrúðnir
"Dellingr heitir,
hann er Dags faðir,
en Nótt var Nörvi borin;
ný ok nið
skópu nýt regin
öldum at ártali."

Vafthrudnir
"Dellingr is named
he who is Dagr's father,
but night was of Norvi born;
new and waning
creation produced
waves to reckon years."

Forseti (God of Justice and Reconciliation)

Forseti is a member of the *Æsir*. In Old Norse his name means 'the presiding one' or 'president', literally 'one who sits before'. The word is still used meaning president in modern Icelandic and Faroese.

The name and its meaning can also be similarly found in the Old English '*fore-sittan*', possibly the Old High German '**forasizo*', and the modern German '*Vorsitzender*'.

The word 'president' is composed in the same way from the Latin '*praesidentum*' ('*prae*' = 'before' + '*sedere*' = 'to sit').

Forseti is the son of Baldr and Nanna. He has great skill in mediation, putting to sleep all suits and stilling all strifes. Everyone who comes to him with even the most difficult of law-disputes goes away satisfied.

Forseti is generally identified with Fosite, a god worshipped by the Frisians. According to Alcuin's Life of St Willebrond, the saint visited an island between Frisia and Denmark that was sacred to Fosite and it was called Fositesland after the god worshipped there.

There is also a late-medieval legend of the origins of written Frisian laws. Wishing to assemble written lawcodes for all his subjects, Charlemagne summoned twelve representatives of the Frisians, known as the '*asegas*' ('law-speakers'). He demanded that they recite their people's laws. When they could not do so after several days, he let them choose between death, slavery, or being set adrift in a rudderless boat. They chose the last option and prayed for help.

A thirteenth man appeared with a golden axe on his shoulder. He steered the boat to land with his axe, and then threw the axe ashore, and a spring appeared where the axe had landed. He taught them laws and then disappeared. The stranger and the spring have been traditionally identified with Fosite and the sacred spring of Fositesland.

On the island the sacred spring was so holy, that water had to be drawn from it in silence. Adam of Bremen tells the same story and adds that the island is called *Heiligland* ('holy land') i.e. Heligoland.

Forseti also seems to have been worshipped in a place called *Forsetlund* (Old Norse: *Forsetalundr*) a farm in the parish of *Onsøy* ('Odin's Island'), in eastern Norway.

Forseti's home is called *Glitnir* ('the shining') with gold pillars and a roof made of silver which radiates light that can be seen from far and wide, it is the seat of justice amongst gods and men.

Forseti is mentioned in the *Poetic Edda* in *Grímnismál* ('The Lay of Grimnir'), a poem spoken from the perspective of Grimnir, one of the many guises of Odin.

*15. Glitnir er inn tíundi, hann er gulli studdr
ok silfri þakðr it sama;
en þar Forseti byggir flestan dag
ok svæfir allar sakir.*

15. Glitnir is the tenth, it is gold in pillars
And covered with silver the same;
And there Forseti dwells most of his days
And puts to sleep all strife.

Forseti is also mentioned in the the *Prose Edda* in *Gylfaginning* ('The Beguiling of Gylfi'):

*"Forseti heitir sonur Baldurs og Nönnu Nepsdóttur.
Hann á þann sal á himni er Glitnir heitir.*

*En allir er til hans koma með sakarvandræði, þá fara allir sáttir á braut.
Sá er dómstaður bestur með guðum og mönnum. Svo segir hér:*

*Glitnir heitir salur,
hann er gulli studdur
og silfri þaktur hið sama;
en þar Forseti
byggir flestan dag
og svæfir allar sakar."*

"Forseti is named the son of Baldr and Nanna daughter of Nep.
He has that hall in heaven which Glitnir is named.

And all that to him come with troublesome cases, then go all happily away.
So is the place of judgment the best among gods and men. So it says here:

Glitnir is named a hall,
it is gold pillared
and silver covered the same;
and there Forseti
dwells most of his days
and puts to sleep all disputes."

Forseti's role as a mediator of gods and men is symbolic in presenting the importance of discussion in the resolution of conflict rather than violence.

Forseti Seated in Judgment by Carl Emil Doepler, 1881
Creative Commons, Public Domain

Heimdall (God of Light, Watchman of the Gods)

Heimdall (Heimdallr, Heimdallur, also known as Rig, Hallinskiði, Gullintanni, Vindlér or Vindhlér) is a member of the *Æsir*.

He is associated with light and prophecy, and he keeps watch for invaders, and for the onset of *Ragnarök* ('the Twilight of the Gods'), from his dwelling called *Himinbjörg* ('heaven's castle' or 'heaven's mountain') in which he has a store of fine mead.

In the *Prose Edda*, *Himinbjörg* is described as being located where *Bifröst* ('the burning rainbow bridge') meets the heavens.

Heimdall is the son of Odin and the Nine Mothers of Heimdall. They are nine sisters who were born of Ægir and Rán (personifications of the sea) who all gave birth to Heimdall together, and are often depicted as waves, implying that Heimdall is born of the sea.

Heimdall is described as having foreknowledge and keen senses, particularly eyesight and hearing. He has golden teeth, and he is described as the whitest of gods.

He has a horse called *Gulltopr* ('golden mane'). He also owns the horn called *Gjallarhorn* ('loud sounding horn') whose sound is so loud that when blown it will be heard in all corners of the world, and it will herald the beginning of *Ragnarök* ('the Twilight of the Gods').

In the *Poetic Edda* in *Völuspá* ('The Prophecy of the Völva'), the undead völva (seeress) calls out for the listeners to be silent, and refers to Heimdall.

"Hljóðs bið ek allar helgar kindir,
meiri ok minni mögu Heimdallar;
viltu at ek, Valföðr,
vel fyr telja forn spjöll fira,
þau er fremst of man."

"Silence, I bid you all holy children,
More and less may Heimdall;
They will that I, Valfather (Odin),
Well before telling the ancient spell of men,
Those that are foremost to remember."

In the *Grímnismál* ('The Lay of Grímnir'), Odin (disguised as Grímnir) tells the young Agnar of a number of mythological locations. The eighth location he mentions is *Himinbjörg*, where Heimdall drinks fine mead.

"Himinbjörg eru in áttu, en þar Heimdall
kveða valda véum;
þar vörðr goða drekkr í væru ranni
glaðr inn góða mjöð."

"Himinbjorg is the eigth, and there Heimdall
it is said wields rule;
there the ward of the gods drinks in comfort
gladly the good mead."

In the *Lokasenna* ('Loki's Verbal Duel'), Hemidall asks Loki why he won't stop talking as he is drunk. Loki responds by saying that Heimdall has been fated a hateful life to serve as watchman of the gods.

Heimdallr kvað:
Ǫlr ertu, Loki, svá at þú ert ørviti,

hví né lezkaðu, Loki?
Þvíat ofdrykkja veldr alda hveim,
er sína mælgi né manað!

Loki kvað:
Þegi þú, Heimdallr! Þér var í árdaga
it ljóta líf um lagit;
aurgu baki þú munt æ vera,
ok vaka vǫrðr goða!

Heimdall spoke:
"Drunk are you, Loki, so that you are un-knowing.

Why do you not leave off, Loki?
Because drunkenness rules every man,
Who his neither measured nor mannered!

Loki spoke:
"Be silent, Heimdall! You in early days
Were that hateful life fated:
With a wet back you shall ever be,
And awake ward the gods."

In the *Poetic Edda* in *Þrymskviða* ('Thrym's Poem'), the gods gather to discuss the loss of Thor's hammer *Mjöllnir*. *Mjöllnir* has been stolen by the *jötnar* (giants) and they are demanding the beautiful goddess Freyja in return for *Mjöllnir*. Heimdall advises that they dress Thor up as Freyja:

Þá kvað þat Heimdallr, hvítastr ása,
vissi hann vel fram sem Vanir aðrir:
"Bindum vér Þór þá brúðar líni,
hafi hann it mikla men Brísinga.

Látum und hánum hrynja lukla
ok kvenváðir um kné falla,
en á brjósti breiða steina
ok hagliga um höfuð typpum."

Then Heimdall spoke, whitest of the gods,
Knew he well the future as the other *Vanir*:
"Bind we Thor then a bridal veil,
Have him the mighty Brisings necklace;

"Keys around him let there hang,
And a woman's dress about his knees fall,
With gems broad upon his chest,
And favourably about his head a crown."

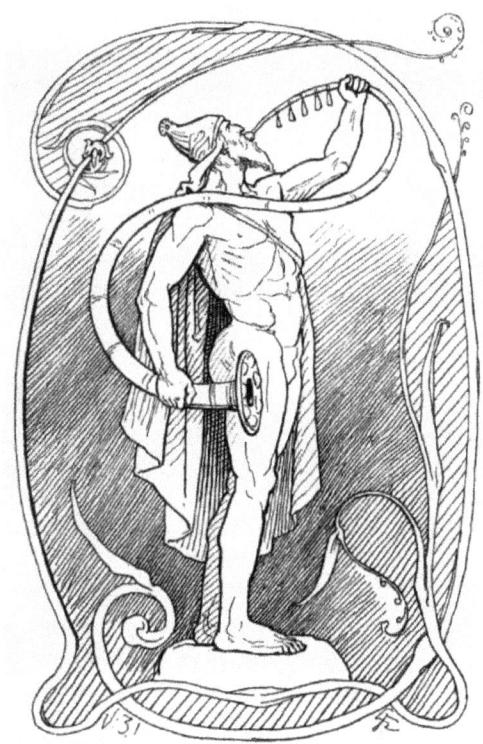

Heimdall blows Gjallarhorn by Lorenz Frølich, 1895
Creative Commons, Public Domain

Hermodr (The Messenger of the Gods)

Hermodr (Hermóðr, Hermóður, Hermod) is a member of the *Æsir*. He is the son of Odin and Frigg, and the brother of Baldr, Bragi, Heimdall, Hodr, Thor, Tyr, Vali, and Vidarr. His name in Old Norse means 'spirit of war'. He is regarded a messenger of the gods largely because of the epic journey that he undertakes to Hel (the underworld) on behalf of Frigg and the whole of the *Æsir*.

In the *Prose Edda* in *Gylfaginning* ('The Beguiling of Gylfi'), the gods are speechless and devastated at the death of Baldr, and are unable to react due to their grief. Eventually, after the gods are able to gather their thoughts from the immense shock and grief, Frigg asks the *Æsir* who among them wishes to "gain all of her love and favour" by riding the road to Hel.

Whoever agrees is to offer Hel a ransom in exchange for Baldr's return. Hermodr volunteers to make the journey and sets off on Odin's grey eight-legged horse *Sleipnir* ('slippy-one'). Hermodr rides Sleipnir for nine days and nights through deep and dark valleys. He comes to the bridge called *Gjallarbrú* ('*Gjöll* bridge') that is thatched with gold and spans the river *Gjöll*, the river which separates the living from the dead.

"Hann reið níu nætr dökkva dala ok djúpa, svá at hann sá ekki, fyrr en hann kom til árinnar Gjallar ok reið á Gjallarbrúna. Hon var þökð lýsigulli."

"He rode nine nights through dark dales and deep, so that he saw not before that came to the river Gjöll and rode onto the Gjöll-Bridge; with which she is thatched with glittering gold."

The *Gjöll* bridge is guarded by the maiden Modgudr (*Móðguðr*, 'battle-frenzy' or 'battle-tired'). Modgudr tells Hermodr that Baldr has already crossed the bridge and that Hermodr should ride downwards and northwards.

"Hann svarar, at -"ek skal ríða til Heljar at leita Baldrs, eða hvárt hefir þú nakkvat sét Baldr á helvegi?"
En hon sagði, at Baldr hafði þar riðit um Gjallarbrú, "en niðr ok norðr liggr helvegr."

"He answered, that - "I shall ride to Hel to seek Baldr, and whether have you something seen of Baldr going Hel-way?"
Then she said, that Baldr has there ridden over Gjallarbrú, but down and north lying Hel-way".

Arriving at Hel's gate, Hermodr makes Sleipnir leap entirely over the gate. When he reaches Hel's hall, he sees Baldr seated in the most honourable seat and stays the night. The next morning, Hermodr begs Hel to release Baldr to return to *Asgard* (the home of the gods), recounting the great sorrow and weeping that his death has caused the *Æsir*.

"Þá reið Hermóðr heim til hallarinnar ok steig af hesti, gekk inn í höllina, sá þar sitja í öndugi, Baldr bróður sinn, ok dvalðist Hermóðr þar um nóttina. En at morgni þá beiddist Hermóðr af Helju, at Baldr skyldi ríða heim með honum, ok sagði, hversu mikill grátr var með ásum."

"Then rode Hermodr home to the hall and dismounted from his horse, went into the hall, saw there sitting in the high-seat, Baldr his brother, and dwelled Hermodr there about the night. In the morning, then begged Hermodr of Hel, that Baldr should ride home with him, and said how so much grief was with the Æsir."

Hel announces that Baldr will only be released if all things, whether dead or alive, weep for him.

"En Hel sagði, at þat skyldi svá reyna, hvárt Baldr var svá ástsæll - "sem sagt er. Ok ef allir hlutir í heiminum, kykvir ok dauðir, gráta hann, þá skal hann fara til ása aftr, en haldast með Helju, ef nakkvarr mælir við eða vill eigi gráta."

"Then Hel said, that it should so be tested, whether Baldr was so all-beloved - "as said was. And if all things in the world, the quick and the dead, weep for him, then shall he travel to the Æsir after, but he shall be held in Hel, if any measure against or will not weep."

Baldr gives Hermodr the ring *Draupnir* ('The-Dripper') which had been burned with him on his funeral pyre, to take back to Odin. Nanna, Baldr's wife who has now joined Baldr, gives Hermodr a linen robe for Frigg along with other gifts, and a finger-ring for Fulla.

"Þá stóð Hermóðr upp, en Baldr leiddi hann út ór höllinni ok tók hringinn Draupni ok sendi Óðni til minja, en Nanna sendi Frigg rifti ok enn fleiri gjafar. Fullu fingrgull."

"Then Hermódr arose; but Baldr led him out of the hall, and took the ring Draupnir and sent it to Odin for remembrance. And Nanna sent Frigg a linen robe, and yet more gifts, and to Fulla a golden finger-ring."

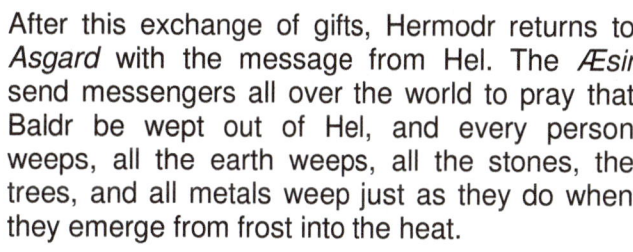

After this exchange of gifts, Hermodr returns to *Asgard* with the message from Hel. The *Æsir* send messengers all over the world to pray that Baldr be wept out of Hel, and every person weeps, all the earth weeps, all the stones, the trees, and all metals weep just as they do when they emerge from frost into the heat.

The messengers believe they have performed their task well, until they find a giantess named Thokk sat in a cave who refuses to weep, declaring *"haldi Hel því, er hefir."* ("let Hel hold on to that which she has.").

Everyone deems that this giantess is Loki in disguise, and Baldr has to remain in the underworld.

Left: An illustration of Hermodr riding Sleipnir to Baldr in Hel
NKS 1867 4to, 96r, 1760
Creative Commons, Public Domain

Hodr (God of Winter, Cold, and Darkness)

Hodr (Hǫðr, Höðr, Höður) is a member of the *Æsir*. He is the son of Odin and Frigg, and the brother of Baldr, Bragi, Heimdall, Hermodr, Thor, Tyr, Vali, and Vidarr.

His name can be translated as 'warrior' from the Old Norse '*hǫð*' ('war' or 'slaughter'), the Old English '*heaðu-deór*' ('brave', 'stout in war'), the Old High German '*hadu-*', the Old Saxon '*hathu-*', the Old Frisian '*-had*', and the Burgundian '**haþus*', all originating from the Proto-Germanic '**haþuz*' ('battle').

In the *Prose Edda* in *Gylfaginning* ('The Beguiling of Gylfi'), Hodr is introduced:

"Höðr heitir einn ássinn, hann er blindr. Œrit er hann styrkr, en vilja mundu goðin at þenna ás þyrfti eigi at nefna, því at hans handaverk munu lengi vera höfð at minnum með goðum ok mönnum."

"Hodr is named one of the *Æsir*, he is blind. Sufficient is he in strength, but wish will the gods that this god of the *Æsir* is not to be named, because his handiwork shall long be in the head of memory with the gods and men."

Hodr is not mentioned again until the prelude to Baldr's death is described:

En Loki tók mistiltein ok sleit upp ok gekk til þings.
En Höðr stóð útarliga í mannhringinum, því at hann var blindr.
Þá mælti Loki við hann: "Hví skýtr þú ekki at Baldri?"
Hann svarar: "Því at ek sé eigi hvar Baldr er, ok þat annat at ek em vápnlauss."
Þá mælti Loki: "Gerðu þó í líking annarra manna ok veit Baldri sœmð sem aðrir menn.

Ek mun vísa þér til hvar hann stendr. Skjót at honum vendi þessum."
Höðr tók mistiltein ok skaut at Baldri at tilvísun Loka.
Flaug skotit í gögnum hann ok fell hann dauðr til jarðar.
Ok hefir þat mest óhapp verit unnit með goðum ok mönnum.

"Then Loki took the mistletoe and pulled it up and went to the assembly.
Then Hodr stood outer-lying the ring of people, because he was blind.
Then spoke Loki with him: "Why shoot you not at Baldr?"
He answered: "Because I see not where Baldr is, and it also is that I am weaponless".
Then spoke Loki: "Do you though alike to other men and show Baldr honour as other men.
I shall see you to where he stands. Shoot at him this wand."
Hodr took the mistletoe and shot at Baldr with the guidance of Loki.
The shaft shot and got him and fell he dead to the earth.
And has this the greatest mishap that has befallen with gods and men.

The gods were stunned into silence and inaction, none of them were able to speak, act, or avenge Baldr's death in such a place.

> *"Þá er Baldr var fallinn, þá fellusk öllum ásum orðtök ok svá hendr at taka til hans, ok sá hverr til annars ok váru allir með einum hug til þess er unnit hafði verkit. En engi mátti hefna, þar var svá mikill griðastaðr."*

> "Then when Balder was fallen, then failed all of the *Æsir* in taking to words, and so to taking his hand, and looked each to each other, and were they all in one thought to this whose work it was. But none may avenge, there was so much a sanctuary".

Odin and Rindr (a giantess, goddess, or human princess) give birth to Vali who grows to adulthood in a single day and slays Hodr as punishment for killing his own brother.

> *"Hvernig skal kenna Vála? Svá, at kalla hann son Óðins ok Rindar, stjúpson Friggjar, bróður ásanna, hefniás Baldrs, dólg Haðar ok bana hans, byggvanda föðurtófta."*

> "How shall be known Vali? So, that call him son Odin's and Rindr, stepson of Frigg, brother of the *Æsir*, avenger of Baldr, foe of Hodr and his slayer, dweller in the fathers homesteads."

The death of Baldr is a tragedy, and an additional layer of complexity to this tradgedy is the way in which Hodr is punished and killed in avenging Baldr's death. The mistletoe was indeed fired by his hands, but he is clearly innocent and cruelly tricked by Loki. Such a tragic series of events is symbolic of the disruptive forces of the universe that Loki comes to represent with his anarchy and antagonism. It is perhaps a cautionary tale warning its audience to beware the motives of those who would compel their actions with evil intent.

Guided and deceived by Loki, the blind god Hodr throws a spear of mistletoe at Baldr, killing him.
Illustration by Carl Emil Doepler, 1882
Creative Commons, Public Domain

Hoenir (God of Silence and Spirituality)

Hoenir (Hœnir, Hænir, Höner, Hǿnir) is a member of the *Æsir*. He is the son of Borr and Bestla, and he is the brother of Odin, Villi, and Ve. Hoenir is mentioned in the *Poetic Edda* in *Völuspá* ('The Prophecy of the Völva') as one of the three gods (along with Odin and Lodurr) that created the first humans, Ask and Embla. Hoenir is credited with having given sense to the first humans (In the *Prose Edda*, this act is performed by Odin, Vili, and Ve).

17. Unz þrír kvámu ór því liði öflgir ok ástgir Æsir at húsi, fundu á landi lítt megandi Ask ok Emblu örlöglausa.	17. Until three came out of that company mighty and loving Æsir to a house, found they on land little capable Ask and Embla destiny-less.
18. Önd þau né áttu, óð þau né höfðu, lá né læti né litu góða. Önd gaf Óðinn, óð gaf Hœnir, lá gaf Lóðurr ok litu góða.	18. Spirit they did not have, sense they did not have, blood nor mannerisms, nor good colour. spirit gave Odin, sense gave Hoenir, blood gave Lodurr, and good colour.

The *Völuspá* also predicts that Hoenir will be one of the few gods to survive *Ragnarök* ('the Twilight of the Gods').

Hoenir is mentioned in Snorri Sturluson's *Heimskringla*, in the *Ynglinga Saga* ('the Saga of the Ynlings'), a work based on the older *Ynlingatal* ('the Account of the Ynglings') attributed to the 9th century Norwegian skald Thjodolf of Hvinir. It tells the story of the arrival of the gods in Scandinavia, and the founding of the *Yngling Dynasty* by Freyr and Gerdr and the descent of the kings of Norway from the royal house of Sweden.

After the *Æsir-Vanir* War, the gods appoint a meeting to establish peace, call a truce, and exchange hostages. The *Vanir* send their best men, Njord the Rich and his son Freyr. The *Æsir* send Hoenir, who they believe is suitable as a chief, and Mimir (Mímir), who is "of great understanding". On arrival in *Vanaheim* (the home of the *Vanir*), Hoenir is made a chief, but relies on Mimir for decision making, offering non-commital answers when Mimir is absent.

En er Hœnir kom í Vanaheim, þá var hann þegar höfðingi gerr; Mímir kendi honum ráð öll.	And when Hoenir came to Vanaheim he was immediately made a chief, and Mimir came to him with good counsel on all occasions.
En er Hœnir var staddr á þingum eða stefnum, svá at Mímir var eigi nær, ok kœmi nökkur vandamál fyrir hann, þá svaraði hann æ hinu sama: ráði aðrir, sagði hann.	But when Hoenir stood in the assemblies or other meetings, if Mimir was not near him, and any difficult matter was laid before him, he always answered in one way -- "Now let others give their advice";
Þá grunaði Vani, at Æsir mundi hafa falsat þá í mannaskiptinu; þá tóku þeir Mími ok hálshjoggu ok sendu höfuðit Ásum.	So the *Vanir* got a suspicion that the *Æsir* had deceived them in the exchange of men. They took Mimir, therefore, and beheaded him, and sent his head to the *Æsir*.
Óðinn tók höfuðit ok smurði urtum, þeim er eigi mátti fúna, ok kvað þar yfir galdra, ok magnaði svá, at þat mælti við hann ok sagði honum marga leynda hluti.	Odin took the head, smeared it with herbs so that it should not rot, and sang incantations over it. Thereby he gave it the power that it spoke to him, and discovered to him many secrets.

Hoenir, Lóðurr and Odin create Askr and Embla by Lorenz Frølich, 1895
Creative Commons, Public Domain

Lodurr (Creator of Humans)

Lodurr (Lóðurr) is mentioned in the *Poetic Edda* in *Völuspá* ('The Prophecy of the Völva') as one of the three gods (along with Odin and Hoenir) that created the first humans, Ask and Embla. Hoenir is credited with having given the first humans "blood" and "good colour" (In the *Prose Edda*, this act is performed by Odin, Vili, and Ve).

17. Unz þrír kvámu *ór því liði* *öflgir ok ástgir* *Æsir at húsi,* *fundu á landi* *lítt megandi* *Ask ok Emblu* *örlöglausa.*	17. Until three came out of that company mighty and loving *Æsir* to a house, found they on land little capable Ask and Embla destiny-less.
18. Önd þau né áttu, *óð þau né höfðu,* *lá né læti* *né litu góða.* *Önd gaf Óðinn,* *óð gaf Hœnir,* *lá gaf Lóðurr* *ok litu góða.*	18. Spirit they did not have, sense they did not have, blood nor mannerisms, nor colour good. spirit gave Odin, sense gave Hoenir, blood gave Lóðurr, and good colour.

Loki (God of Trickery)

Loki (sometimes Loptr) is a cunning god who is known for his trickery, sowing discord and disruption, and ultimately bringing about the events of *Ragnarök* ('the Twilight of the Gods').

Modern Scandinavian versions of the name Loki (Faroese: *Lokki*, Danish: *Lokkemand*, Norwegian: *Loke* or *Lokke*, Swedish: *Luki* or *Luku*) point to an origin in the Germanic root '*luk-*', which denotes things to do with loops, knots, hooks, and locks. This suggests that he is a cause of knots, tangles, or loops, or that he is himself a knot, tangle, or loop.

It is worth noting that likely from the same Germanic root, the Icelandic word '*lok*' (which corresponds with the word 'lock' in English) can also mean 'completion' or 'ending', which some have suggested points to his name possibly meaning 'he who brings about the end', symbolising his role in the ending of the world in the events of *Ragnarök* ('the Twilight of the Gods').

His name also appears as *Loptr*, from the Old Norse lopt meaning 'air', which points to an association with the air.

Loki is the son of the *jötunn* (giant) Fárbauti, and Laufey (or Nál), a goddess. With the goddess Sigyn he is the father of Vali (not to be confused with Odin's son of the same name) and Narfi. With the *jötunn* (giant) Angrboða he is the father of Fenrir (a giant wolf), Jörmungandr (the giant serpent who encircles the earth), and Hel (the keeper of the underworld).

While in the form of a mare, Loki is impregnated by the stallion Svadilfari and gives birth to Odin's grey eight-legged horse Sleipnir ('slippy-one'). He has also been known to shape-shift into a salmon, a mare, a fly, a falcon, an elderly woman, and possibly a giantess named Thokk (Þökk, Old Norse: 'thanks').

Loki's positive interaction with the gods comes to an end with his role in the death of Baldr. Not only is Loki responsible for Baldr's death, he is also responsible for Hodr's death, whom he tricks into firing the shaft of mistletoe that kills Baldr, for which Hodr is killed as punishment. Not only that, but Loki actively disrupts any hope of Baldr being released from the underworld by disguising himself as an old giantess who refuses to weep for Baldr, thus condemning Baldr to remain in the underworld.

In the *Poetic Edda* in *Lokasenna* ('Loki's Verbal Duel'), Loki throws a series of barbed insults at the gods during a feast in Ægir's hall, in an attempt to create discord and to "mix their mead with malice".

Loki is punished for his wrong doing and his taunting by being bound by the entrails of one of his sons, while goddess Skadi holds a giant serpent above his head. The serpent drips venom from above him, which his wife Sigyn collects into a bowl. Each time Sigyn has to empty the bowl, the venom drips into Loki's eyes, causing him unimaginable pain, at which he writhes in agony causing the earth to shake in the process.

It is foretold that Loki will eventually break free from his bonds and join the forces of the *jötnar* (giants), to go to battle with the gods, and fight a duel with Heimdall. Meanwhile, Loki's offspring play a key role in the destruction of all but two humans during the events of *Ragnarök* ('the Twilight of the Gods').

In the *Poetic Edda* in *Völuspá* ('The Prophecy of the Völva'), the völva (seeress) sees Sigyn sitting unhappily with her bound husband Loki under a "grove of hot springs".

35. Haft sá hon liggja und Hveralundi, lægjarns líki Loka áþekkjan; þar sitr Sigyn þeygi of sínum ver vel glýjuð. Vituð ér enn - eða hvat?	35. She has seen lying under hot spring groves, humbled body Loki similar to; there sits Sigyn though not glad or well gleeful. Do you understand, or what?

Later on she also sees Loki free from his bonds and steering a ship containing the fire giants with his brother Býleistr, on their way to the final battle with the gods.

Kjóll ferr austan, koma munu Múspells of lög lýðir, en Loki stýrir; fara fíflmegir með freka allir, þeim er bróðir Býleists í för.	A keel travels from the east, they will be coming from Muspelheim with flame lying, and Loki is steering; travelling monsters with wildness all, them his brother Býleistr travels with.

An illustration of Loki
SÁM 66, c. 1765-1766
Creative Commons, Public Domain

Mani (God of the Moon)

Mani (Old Norse: Máni) is the personification of the moon. His name literally means 'moon'. His sister is Sól (the personofication of the sun), and they are the son and daughter of Mundilfari ('the one moving according to particular times'). Mani crosses the sky every night in a horse-drawn carriage, and he is followed by the sister and brother Bil and Hjuki. Scholars discuss and debate the nature of Bil and Hjuki, arguing in favour of their role as potential personifications of the craters on the Moon or its phases. The story goes that they were fetching water from the well called Byrgir ('hider of something'), carrying a pole on their shoulders called Simul, and a pail called Saeg, when Mani took them from the earth and into the heavens where they now follow him.

"Máni stýrir göngu tungls ok ræðr nýjum ok niðum. Hann tók tvau börn af jörðunni, er svá heita, Bil ok Hjúki, er þau gengu frá brunni þeim er, Byrgir heitir, ok báru á öxlum sér sá, er heitir Sægr, en stöngin Simul. Viðfinnr er nefndr faðir þeira. Þessi börn fylgja Mána, svá sem sjá má af jörðu."	"Mani steers the course of the moon, and determines its waxing and waning. He took two children from the earth, who are named Bil and Hjuki, as they went from the spring that is named Byrgr, and the bore a pole which is named Saeg, and the pole Simul. Vidfinn is their father named. The children follow Mani, so as seen may be from earth."

In his journey across the night sky, Mani is chased by the Great Wolf called Hati, who catches and devours him during the events of *Ragnarök* ('The Twilight of the Gods'). Mani is potentially connected to the idea of the Man in the Moon, which appears in many cultures across Northern Europe. Some Germanic cultures describe the Man in the Moon as a woodcutter who was caught working on the Sabbath and banished to the night sky.

Mimir (God of Wisdom)

Mimir is a god who is renowned for his knowledge and wisdom. He drinks regularly from his own well called Mímisbrunnr ('Mimir's Wellspring') which gives him his knowledge and wisdom.

Mímisbrunnr is located in Jötunheimr ('The Ream of the Giants', literally 'Giant-Home') where the primordial plane of Ginnungagap ('gaping abyss', 'yawning void') once existed at the beginning of creation. It is one of the three wells that support three large roots of Yggdrasil ('The World Tree').

After the *Æsir-Vanir* War, the gods appoint a meeting to establish peace, call a truce, and exchange hostages. The *Vanir* send their best men, Njord the Rich and his son Freyr. The *Æsir* send Hoenir, who they believe is suitable as a chief, and Mimir (Old Norse: Mímir), who is a man of great understanding.

On arrival in Vanaheim, Hoenir is made a chief, but relies on Mimir for decision making, offering non-commital answers when Mimir is absent. The *Æsir* behead Mimir, but Odin keeps his head which continues to talk to Odin giving him wisdom and wise counsel.

En er Hœnir kom í Vanaheim, þá var hann þegar höfðingi gerr; Mímir kendi honum ráð öll.

And when Hoenir came to Vanaheim he was immediately made a chief, and Mimir came to him with good counsel on all occasions.

En er Hœnir var staddr á þingum eða stefnum, svá at Mímir var eigi nær, ok kœmi nökkur vandamál fyrir hann, þá svaraði hann æ hinu sama: ráði aðrir, sagði hann.

But when Hoenir stood in the assemblies or other meetings, if Mimir was not near him, and any difficult matter was laid before him, he always answered in one way -- "Now let others give their advice";

Þá grunaði Vani, at Æsir mundi hafa falsat þá í mannaskiptinu; þá tóku þeir Mími ok hálshjoggu ok sendu höfuðit Ásum.

so that the *Vanir* got a suspicion that the *Æsir* had deceived them in the exchange of men. They took Mimir, therefore, and beheaded him, and sent his head to the *Æsir*.

Óðinn tók höfuðit ok smurði urtum, þeim er eigi mátti fúna, ok kvað þar yfir galdra, ok magnaði svá, at þat mælti við hann ok sagði honum marga leynda hluti.

Odin took the head, smeared it with herbs so that it should not rot, and sang incantations over it. Thereby he gave it the power that it spoke to him, and discovered to him many secrets.

Modi and Magni (The Wrathful and Mighty Sons of Thor)

Modi (Móði, Módi, Mothi, 'Wrath') and Magni ('Mighty') are the sons of Thor, and the brothers of Thrudr (Þrúðr, 'Strength'). Thor fathered Modi and Thrudr with the goddess Sif, and Magni with the *jötunn* (giant) Jarnsaxa (Járnsaxa, 'Iron Dagger').

Modi and Magni are mentioned among the survivors of *Ragnarök* ('The Twilight of the Gods') in the *Poetic Edda* in *Vafþrúðnismál* ('The Lay of Vafþrúðnir').

It is said that they shall own Thor's hammer, Mjolnir, after their father Thor dies (having killed the world serpent Jormungandr only to succumb to Jormungandr's poisonous venom nine steps later).

*"Móði ok Magni
skulu Mjöllni hafa
Vingnis at vígþroti."*

"Modi and Magni
shall Mjollnir have
when Vingnir (Thor) is fight-fallen."

In *Skáldskaparmál* ('The Language of Poetry'), Magni plays a role in the story of Thor's battle with the giant Hrungnir ('Brawler', 'Big Person', 'Strong Man', 'Noise-Maker').

While Odin is riding home to Asgard (Old Norse: Ásgarðr; 'enclosure of the *Æsir*'), he encounters a giant named Hrungnir. They engage in conversation about the quality of their horses, and then engage in a wager to see who has the fastest horse. Odin stakes his head that his horse Sleipnir ('The Slippy One') is faster than Hrungnir's horse Gullfaxi ('Golden-Mane').

Odin and Hrungnir race back towards Asgard. Sleipnir wins the race, but Hrungnir is too close behind to be prevented from entering Asgard, where he becomes drunk and abusive.

The gods grow weary of Hrungnir and call upon Thor to do battle with him. Thor strikes Hrungnir in the middle of his head with his hammer Mjolnir, shattering it into small crumbs.

A now headless Hrungnir falls on top of Thor so that his foot lies over Thor's neck. All of the gods try to lift Hrungnir's foot off Thor's neck, but none of them have enough strength to succeed.

Then Magni, who is only three nights old at this point, arrives and succeeds in lifting Hrungnir's foot off Thor's neck, saying to his father: "See how ill it is, father, that I came so late. I would have struck this giant dead with my fist, I think, if I had met with him".

Thor arose and welcomed his son and said that he would surely become great. Thor then gave Hrungnir's horse Gullfaxi to Magni. Odin then spoke and said that Thor had done wrong to give the good horse to the son of a giantess instead of his father.

Odin (The Allfather)

Odin (Old Norse: Óðinn, also Woden or Wotan) is a member of the *Æsir*. He is the son of Borr and Bestla, and the brother of Vili, Ve, and Hoenir, the husband of Frigg, and the father of Baldr, Bragi, Heimdall, Hermodr, Hodr, Tyr, Vali, and Vidarr.

With the goddess Jord (Jörð or Fjörgyn) he is also the father of the god Thor. He is associated with wisdom, healing, death, royalty, the gallows, knowledge, war, battle, victory, sorcery, poetry, frenzy, and the runic alphabet.

Odin is widely revered in Germanic paganism, known in Old English as Wōden, in Old Saxon as Uuôden, in Old Dutch as Wuodan, in Old Frisian as Wêda, and in Old High German as Wuotan, all coming from the Proto-Germanic '*Wōðanaz*', meaning 'lord of frenzy', or 'leader of the possessed'.

He is a prominent god throughout the history of mythology and rural folklore in Northern Europe, from the Roman occupations of Germania (2 BCE), the Migration Period (4th to 6th centuries CE), and through the Viking Age (8th to 11th centuries CE) and beyond.

The modern English weekday Wednesday is named after him, from the Old Norse Oðinsdagr, Old English wodnesdæg ('Woden's day'), Danish, Norwegian, and Swedish Onsdag, Old Frisian Wonsdei, and Middle Dutch Wudensdach. The Latin equivalent name for Wednesday is Mercuri Dies ('Day of Mercury'), which became the French mercredi, Italian mercoledi, and Spanish miércoles. Among the many associations of the god Mercury are divine messenger, wanderer, traveller, which are comparable to aspects of Odin.

The Roman historian Tacitus in his first century work Germania writes about the religion of the Germanic peoples, including the confederation of tribes known as the Suebi. He comments that among their many gods, Mercury (Odin, '*Wōðanaz*') is the one that they principally worship by offering sacrifices on fixed days. He also mentions the worship of Hercules, and Isis, which are interpreted as Roman equivalents of Thor ('*Þunraz*') and Tyr ('*Tīwaz*') respectively.

In old texts and poetry he is referred to by over 170 different names, nicknames, and kenningar. Perhaps the best known of these names is the Old Norse Aldafaðr ('father of men') or Alfǫðr ('the all-father'). He also frequently disguises himself under many different names.

He is commonly depicted with a long beard, with one eye, wielding a spear named Gungnir ('The Swaying One'), wearing a cloak and a broad hat. He is often accompanied by his animal familiars: The wolves Geri and Freki, and the ravens Huginn and Muninn who bring him information from all across Midgard or Middle Earth. He also rides his grey eight-legged horse Sleipnir ('The Slippery One') across the sky and into the underworld.

Odin is associated with the divine maidens of the battlefield, the Valkyries, who guide half of all the souls from the battlefield to Odin's hall Valhalla, where they feast, tell each other stories of their battle glory, and prepare for the coming of *Ragnarök* ('the Twilight of the Gods'). The other half of the souls go to the goddess Freyja in her meadow or field named Fólkvangr (The Field of the Hosts).

Odin takes part in the creation of the world by slaying the primordial being Ymir and giving life to the first two humans Ask and Embla. He also gives mankind the gift of knowledge of the runic alphabet and its magical properties, which he obtained by sacrificing himself and hanging himself on a tree which is presumed to be Yggdrasil. Odin's wider knowledge of magic was given to him by Freyja, who taughtthe art of seiðr (a kind of magic for seeing and influencing the future) to the Aesir.

In the poem Hávamál ('Sayings of the High One'), Odin offers advice for living, proper conduct, and wisdom, and recounts his self-sacrifice for knowledge of the runes.

138. Veit ek, at ek hekk
vindga meiði á
nætr allar níu,
geiri undaðr
ok gefinn Óðni,
sjalfr sjalfum mér,
á þeim meiði,
er manngi veit
hvers af rótum renn.

139. Við hleifi mik sældu
né við hornigi;
nýsta ek niðr,
nam ek upp rúnar,
æpandi nam,
fell ek aftr þaðan.

138. I know that I hung,
On the windy tree,
For all of nine nights,
Wounded with a spear,
And gave Odin,
Me, myself to.
On that tree,
Which no one knows,
Where the roots run.

139. With a loaf my comfort,
Nor with a drinking horn;
I peered down,
I took up runes,
Loudly learnt,
Then I fell back from there.

An illustration of Odin
SÁM 66, c. 1765-1766
Creative Commons, Public Domain

Odr (The Absent Wanderer and God of Passion or Frenzy)

Odr (Old Norse: Óðr) is the husband of Freyja, and together they have two children, Hnoss ('jewel' or 'gem') and Gersemi ('treasure').

The name Odr in Old Norse derives from a noun, meaning 'mind', 'wit', 'soul', 'sense', and also 'song', and 'poetry'. The name comes from the Proto-Germanic '*wōðaz' meaning 'possessed', 'inspired', 'delirious', and 'raging'. Also related is the Old English wōð ('sound', 'noise', 'voice', 'song'), Old High German wuot ('thrill', 'violent', 'agitation'), and Middle Dutch woet ('rage', 'frenzy'). This suggests that Odr was originally thought of as a god of frenzy or rage.

Odr is frequently absent from Freyja, often away on long journeys, and while he is away from her she cries tears of red gold for him and searches for him under a variety of assumed names, such as Gefn ('the giver'), Hörn ('flaxen-one'), Mardöll ('sea-brightener'), Sýr ('sow'), Vanadís ('the Dis' or 'goddess of fate' of the *Vanir*), and Valfreyja ('Freyja of the slain'). Poetic terms or kennings for Freya include 'Wife of Odr'. A kenning for gold has also been poetically referred to as 'Eye-rain of Odr's Bed-Mate'. This shows how profound Freyja's longing is for her absent husband, and how integral he is to Freyja's identity in poetic terms.

The name Odr is closely connected to Odin (Óðinn) which shares the same root ('*Wōðaz' and '*Wōðanaz' respectively). A trait they share in common is being thought of as a wanderer and a traveller, which suggests that perhaps Odr and Odin were originally connected. Scholars have described Odr as a strange double of Odin, or even an older version of Odin.

Perhaps Odr's long journeys away are triggered by his rage and frenzy, as someone who is restless in their search for knowledge and understanding, going on long journeys looking for answers to questions that trouble him. He is certainly a very mysterious and intriguing figure.

Thor (God of Thunder and Lightning)

Thor (Old Norse: Þórr, Icelandic: Þór) is a member of the Aesir. He is the god of lightning, thunder, storms, sacred groves and trees, strength, and the protection of mankind. He is known for being bold, brave, and fearless, and for slaying countless enemies of the gods, including giants and gigantic beasts.

He is also known in Old English as Þunor, in Old Frisian as Thuner, in Old Saxon as Thunar, and in Old High German as Donar, all ultimately stemming from the Proto-Norse '*Þunarr' or '*Þunurr', and the Proto-Germanic '*Þunraz' or '*Þunaraz', meaning Thunder.

Also like Odin, Thor has a number of other names, nicknames, or kennings that have been used to refer to him in poetry and literature, such as Ásabragr (*Æsir*-lord), Björn (bear), Einriði or Eindriði (he who rides alone), and Harðhugaðr (strong spirit, powerful soul, and brave heart).

The modern English weekday name Thursday comes from his name, via the Old Norse Þórsdagr (Thor's day), the Old English þunresdæġ, and Old High German Donaresdag, all of which come from Late Proto-Germanic as '*Þunaresdagaz' (Day of '*Þunaraz'). The equivalent weekday name in Romance languages comes from the Latin Iovis Dies (day of Jove or Jupiter) which became the Italian giovedì, French jeudi, and Spanish jueves. Jupiter is often named as the Roman equivalent of Thor, (and to a lesser extent so is Hercules, as in Tacitus's first century work Germania).

Thor is often depicted wielding his hammer Mjolnir (Old Norse: Mjǫllnir, Icelandic: Mjölnir), which he uses both as a devastating weapon and as a divine instrument to provide blessings. Theories on the origin and meaning of the name Mjolnir are varied. One theory points to the Old Norse word mjǫll (new snow) and the modern Icelandic mjalli (white), suggesting that Mjolnir means a shining lightning weapon.

Thor rides a chariot pulled by two goats Tanngrisnir (teeth-grinder) and Tanngnjóstr (teeth-thin). He has three three dwellings, Bilskirnir (lightning-crack), Þrúðheimr (word of strength), and Þrúðvangr (power-field). He has a belt called Megingjörð (power-belt) which doubles his strength when he wears it, and a pair of iron gloves called Járngreipr (iron-grip). He owns a staff called Gríðarvölr (staff of Gríðr) which the giantess Gríðr lends to him when he needs to cross the river Vimur.

He is the son of Odin and Jord (Jörð or Fjörgyn), and the husband of Sif, and the father of sons Móði, Magni (with Sif), and daughter Þrúðr with the *jötunn* (giant) Járnsaxa. He is also the stepfather of the god Ullr. By way of his father Odin, Thor has many brothers, including Baldr, Bragi, Heimdall, Hermodr, Hodr, Tyr, Vali, and Vidarr.

Like Odin, Thor is a prominently mentioned god throughout the history of the Germanic peoples, from the Roman occupation of the regions of Germania, to the Migration Period, the Viking Age, and long into the Christianisation of Scandinavia. Many personal names based on the name Thor have survived into modern times in Germanic countries.

Archaeologists have discovered petroglyphs featuring a figure holding a hammer-like object, such as the rock carvings in Tanum (Tanumshede, Bohuslän, Sweden), dating back to the Nordic Bronze Age (around 2000 to 500 BCE). Over a thousand pendants representing Thor's hammer Mjolnir have been found by archaeologists in Scandinavia, England, northern Germany, the Baltic countries, and Russia dating back over a thousand years. Such pendants are still worn by pagans today.

In the 11th century, chronicler Adam of Bremen records in his Gesta Hammaburgensis Ecclesiae Pontificum (The Deeds of the Bishops of Hamburg) that sacrifices were made to Thor when plague or famine threatened.

In the *Poetic Edda* in *Völuspá* ('The Prophecy of the Völva'), a völva recounts the history of the universe and foretells the future to a disguised Odin, including the death of Thor. The völva foretells that Thor will do battle with the great serpent Jörmungandr during the events of *Ragnarök* ('the Twilight of the Gods'), and there he will slay the monstrous snake, yet afterwards he will only be able to take nine steps before succumbing to the venom of the beast.

56	*56*
Þá kemr inn mæri	Then comes the noble
mögr Hlóðynjar,	son of Hlóðyn (the earth),
gengr Óðins sonr	goes Odin's son
við orm vega,	against the serpent to slay,
drepr af móði	kills of rage
Miðgarðs véurr,	Midgard's Veor (Thor),
munu halir allir	should all flee
heimstöð ryðja;	homestead free;
gengr fet níu	walking steps nine
Fjörgynjar burr	Mother earth's son (Thor)
neppr frá naðri	overcome from the serpent
níðs ókvíðnum.	down fearless.

The völva then says that afterwards, the sky will turn black before fire engulfs the world, the stars will disappear, flames will dance before the sky, steam will rise, the world will be covered in water and then it will be raised again, green and fertile.

The final battle between Thor and Jörmungandr during *Ragnarök*
by Lorenz Frølich, 1895
Creative Commons, Public Domain.

Tyr (God of War, Warriors, Law, and Justice)

Tyr (Old Norse: Týr) is a member of the Æsir. He is a god of war, warriors, and bravery, particularly bravery on the battlefield. He is also associated with the assembly, law, and justice.

According to *Skáldskaparmál* ('The Language of Poetry'), Tyr is one of Odin's sons, and therefore the brother of Baldr, Bragi, Heimdall, Hermodr, Hodr, Thor, Vali, and Vidarr. Other sources such as the *Hymiskviða* ('The Lay of Hymir') alternatively describe Tyr as the son of *jötunn* (giant) Hymir.

Tyr is known in Old English as Tīw, in Old High German as Ziu, from the Proto-Norse, and Proto-Germanic *'*Tīwaz'*, meaning god or a god. In Old Norse poetry, the plural tívar is used for the gods.

The modern English weekday Tuesday is named after him, from the Old Norse Týsdagr (day of Tyr), the Old English Tīwesdæg, Old Frisian Tīesdi, Old High German Ziostag, Middle High German Zīstac, all of which come from the Late Proto-Germanic *'*Tīwasdag'* (Day of *'*Tīwaz'*).

The Romans identified Tyr with their god Mars. The Latin equivalent of Tuesday is Martis Dies (Day of Mars) which became the Italian martedì, the French mardi, and the Spanish martes.

The Roman historian Tacitus in his first century work Germania writes about the religion of the Germanic peoples, including the confederation of tribes known as the Suebi. Along with Odin (*'*Wōđanaz'*, who he equates as Mercury), Tacitus mentions the worship of Hercules, and Isis, which are interpreted as Roman equivalents of Thor (*'*Þunraz'*) and Tyr (*'*Tīwaz'*) respectively.

In the *Poetic Edda* in Sigrdrífumál ('The Ballad of the Victorious One'), the Valkyrie Sigrdrífa gives the hero Sigurd knowledge of various runic charms, one of which invokes the god Tyr:

> "Sigrúnar skaltu kunna, ef þú vilt sigr hafa, ok rísta á hjalti hjörs, sumar á véttrimum, sumar á valböstum, ok nefna tysvar Tý."

> "Victory-runes shall you know, if you wish victory to have, and cut in the hilt of your sword, some on the blade-ridge, some on the blades, and name twice Tyr."

In the *Prose Edda* in Gylfaginning ('The Beguiling of Gylfi'), the gods are troubled by their knowledge of prophecies foretelling great trouble from the wolf Fenrir (Loki's offspring) and his rapid growth. It is foretold that Fenrir will kill Odin and assist in setting the world on fire.

The Æsir attempt to lure Fenrir in order to bind him with an iron rope called Gleipnir ('the entangled one' or 'the deceiver'). Tyr places his right hand in Fenrir's mouth as a pledge that the Æsir will let him go. Then when the Æsir refuse to release him, Fenrir bites off Tyr's hand at a location "now called the wolf's joint" (the wrist), causing Tyr to lose his right hand. It was only Tyr who had the courage to approach Fenrir and "give it food", sacrificing his right hand in the process.

Also in the *Poetic Edda* in *Lokasenna* ('Loki's Verbal Duel'), Tyr comes to the defence of Freyr's character after Loki insults him. Tyr replies that although he is missing his right hand, Loki misses Fenrir, who is now bound and will remain so until the events of *Ragnarök* ('the Twilight of the Gods').

Týr kvað: "Freyr er beztr allra ballriða ása görðum í; mey hann né grætir né manns konu ok leysir ór höftum hvern."

Tyr spoke: "Freyr is the best of all bold-riders in the *Æsir*'s courts; a maiden he has not made cry, nor a man's wife, and he frees from fetters each-person."

Loki kvað: "Þegi þú, Týr, þú kunnir aldregi bera tilt með tveim; handar innar hægri mun ek hinnar geta, er þér sleit Fenrir frá."

Loki spoke: "Be silent, Tyr, you have-known never the bearing of agreement between two; the right hand, shall I the other get, that from you Fenrir snapped."

Týr kvað: "Handar em ek vanr, en þú hróðrsvitnis, böl er beggja þrá; ulfgi hefir ok vel, er í böndum skal bíða Ragnarökrs."

Tyr spoke: "A hand I am lacking, but you witness, woe is the desire of both; the wolf is also well, who is in chains and must wait for *Ragnarök*."

In the *Prose Edda* in *Gylfaginning* ('The Beguiling of Gylfi'), Tyr is introduced:

"Sá er enn áss, er Týr heitir. Hann er djarfastr ok bezt hugaðr, ok hann ræðr mjök sigri í orrostum. Á hann er gott at heita hreystimönnum. Þat er orðtak, at sá er týhraustr, er um fram er aðra menn ok ekki sést fyrir. Hann var ok vitr, svá at þat er ok mælt, at sá er týspakr, er vitrastr er."

"There is also one of the *Æsir* called Tyr. He is the bravest and most valiant, and he has great power over victory in battles. It is good for men of bravery to pray to him. There is a saying that a man is Tyr-valiant who surpasses other men and does not hesitate. He was so wise that a man who is clever is said to be Tyr-wise."

In the *Prose Edda* in *Skáldskaparmál* ('The Language of Poetry'), a number of kennings are suggested to poets when referring to Tyr, such as "the one-handed As", "feeder of the wolf", "battle-god", and "son of Odin".

Tyr's death is foreseen during the events of *Ragnarök* ('the Twilight of the Gods'). Garm (Old Norse: Garmr) is the bloodstained hellhound who guards the gates of Hel (the underworld) at a cave called Gnipahellir ('Mountain Cave'). He is described as the most evil creature, and he is to wolves and dogs what Odin is to gods and what Yggdrasil is to trees, i.e. the greatest among them. During the events of *Ragnarök*, Garmr howls loudly before Gnipahellir, his fetters break, and he runs free. He battles fiercely with Tyr and they are the death of each other.

Left: An illustration of Fenrir and Tyr
SÁM 66, c. 1765-1766
Creative Commons, Public Domain

Ullr (God of Winter and Skiing)

Ullr (Icelandic: Ullur, also Oller, Ull, Uller, and sometimes Ullinn) is a member of the *Æsir*. He is the son of the goddess Sif, and the stepson of Thor. He is also the half-brother of Thrudr (Þrúðr), a Valkyrie who serves ale to the Einherjar ('those who fight alone') in Valhalla.

His name comes from the Proto-Germanic *'*wulþuz'* meaning 'glory', comparable to the Gothic noun wulþus and the Old English wuldor meaning 'glory' or 'wealth', all of which come from the Proto-Indo-European *'*wul-tus'* ('sight', 'gaze', 'appearance').

His name has been found in a runic inscription as owlþu-þewaz ('servant of Owlthuz' or 'he who has glorious servants') on a small piece of bronze belonging to a sword found in Thorsberg, Germany around 200 CE.

Many place names in Scandinavia refer to his name, for example in Norway: Ullarhváll ('Ullr's hill') an old farm in Oslo and of Ullevaal Stadion, Ullestad ('Ulle's place') an old farm in Voss., and Ullarnes ('Ullr's headland') an old farm in Rennesøy, and in Sweden: Ulleråker ('Ullr's field') Uppland, Ultuna ('Ullr's town') Uppland, and Ullared ('Ull's clearing') Halland.

This indicates that Ullr was an important god in early Germanic paganism long before the Viking Age, even though he does not feature prominently in any of the myths in literature handed down to us.

Ullr is mentioned by Saxo Grammaticus in his 12th century work Gesta Danorum ('Deeds of the Danes'), in which Ullr's name is latinised as Ollerus. He is described as a cunning wizard who once ruled the *Æsir* in place of Odin, with magical means of transportation:

"Fama est, illum adeo praestigiarum usu calluisse, ut ad traicienda maria osse, quod diris carminibus obsignavisset, navigii loco uteretur nec eo segnius quam remigio praeiecta aquarum obstacula superaret."

"The report is that he was so clever by the use of tricks, as to cross the seas with a bone, that he had sealed with terrible spells, he would use instead of a boat nor more sluggish than rowing he would overcome the obstacles thrown by the waters."

In the *Poetic Edda* in *Grímnismál* ('The Lay of Grimnir'), the homes of individual gods are described. Ullr's home is named as Ýdalir ('Yew-Dales' or 'Dale of Yew Trees'). The yew tree is associated with the making of bows, which reinforces Ullr's association with archery as a bow-god.

Ullr is referred to as a son of Sif, and a handsome and accomplished skier and warrior in the *Prose Edda* in *Gylfaginning* ('The Beguiling of Gylfi'):

"Ullr heitir einn, sonr Sifjar, stúpsonr Þórs. Hann er bogmaðr svá góðr ok skíðfærr svá, at engi má við hann keppast. Hann er ok fagr álitum ok hefir hermanns atgervi. Á hann er ok gott at heita í einvígi."

"One is named Ullr, son of Sif's, stepson of Thor. He is a bowman so good and a ski-traveller, that none may with him keep. He is also fair in appearance and has warriors accomplishments. Of him it is good to call-upon in single combat".

In the *Prose Edda* in *Skáldskaparmál* ('The Language of Poetry'), Ullr is given several poetic nicknames or kennings, such as 'ski-god', 'bow-god', hunting-god', and 'shield-god', and also a shield can be referred to as 'Ullr's ship' (if there was a tale of Ullr travelling across the sea on his shield, it has since been lost).

An illustration of Ullr
SÁM 66, c. 1765-1766
Creative Commons, Public Domain

Vali (The Divine Avenger)

Vali is a member of the *Æsir*. He is the son of Odin and the female jötun Rindr, and the brother of Baldr, Bragi, Heimdall, Hermodr, Hodr, Thor, Tyr, and Vidarr.

Vali is a great archer and a courageous fighter on the battlefield. In the *Prose Edda* in *Gylfaginning* ('The Beguiling of Gylfi') he is described as "daring in fights, and a most fortunate marksman".

Vali was born for the sole purpose of avenging Baldr's death. He grew to full adulthood within one day of his birth, and slew Hodr as punishment for killing his own brother. The event is foretold in *Baldrs Draumar* (Baldr's Dreams'):

"Rindr ber Vála	"Rindr shall bear Vali
í vestrsölum,	in the western halls,
sá mun Óðins sonr	and so shall Odin's son
einnættr vega:	after one night slay:
hönd of þvær	hand of theirs
né höfuð kembir,	not head shall comb
áðr á bál of berr	before to the pyre of bearing
Baldrs andskota;	Baldr's enemy;
nauðug sagðak,	forced I spoke,
nú mun ek þegja."	now should I be silent."

Vali is also mentioned as avenging Baldr's death in *Völuspá* ('The Prophecy of the Völva'):

31. *"Ek sá Baldri, blóðgum tívur,*	"I saw Baldr, the bleeding god,
Óðins barni, örlög folgin;	Odin's son, destiny followed;

stóð of vaxinn völlum hæri
mjór ok mjök fagr mistilteinn."

stood of grown fields high
slender and much fair mistletoe."

32. *"Varð af þeim meiði, er mær sýndisk,*
harmflaug hættlig, Höðr nam skjóta;
Baldrs bróðir var of borinn snemma,
sá nam Óðins sonr einnættr vega."

"Became of that hurt, which slender seemed
a dangerous shaft, that Hodr shot;
Baldr's brother was born early,
So took Odin's son (Vali) one night to slay."

Vali is present when Loki is punished for his many crimes by being bound in a cave. One of Loki's sons is killed, and his entrails are used to bind Loki to three large stones, whereupon the bindings turn to iron. Differing interpretations of the text regarding this event appear to have opened up the possibility of there being two Valis (one who is Odin's son, and another who is Loki's son). This occurs in the phrase "Vála vígbǫnd" which translates as either "bonds from Vali's act of slaughter" (Vali is the subject) or "bonds from the act of Vali's slaughter" (Vali is either the subject OR the object, unclear).

In the *Poetic Edda* in *Vafþrúðnismál* ('The Lay of Vafþrúðnir'), Vafþrúðnir states that Vali will survive the events of *Ragnarök* ('the Twilight of the Gods') along with his brother Vidarr, and the sons of Thor, Modi and Magni.

"Víðarr ok Váli
byggja vé goða,
þá er sloknar Surta logi,
Móði ok Magni
skulu Mjöllni hafa
Vingnis at vígþroti."

"Vidarr and Vali
the dwelling mansion of the gods,
then when Surta's flame is extinguished,
Modi and Magni
shall Mjöllnir have,
and end the warfare."

Váli by Carl Emil Doepler, 1882
Creative Commons, Public Domain

Vidarr (The Silent Avenger)

Vidarr (Old Norse: Víðarr, sometimes Vidar, Vithar, or Vitharr) is a member of the *Æsir*. He is the god of vengeance.

He is also the son of Odin and the *jötunn* (giant) Gridr (Gríðr), and the brother of Baldr, Bragi, Heimdall, Hermodr, Hodr, Thor, Tyr, and Vali.

In the *Prose Edda* in *Gylfaginning* ('The Beguiling of Gylfi'), Vidarr is introduced as "the silent god", who is almost as strong as Thor:

"Víðarr heitir einn, inn þögli áss. Hann hefir skó þjokkvan. Hann er sterkr, næst því sem Þórr. Af honum hafa goðin mikit traust í allar þrautir."

"Vídarr is the name of one, the silent god. He has a thick shoe. He is nearly as strong as Thor; in him the gods have great trust in all struggles."

Theories have been proposed that Vidarr's silence may be part of a ritual of silence or other abstentions which often accompany acts of vengeance. For example, Vidarr's brother Vali is born for the sole purpose of avenging Baldr's death, and does not wash his hands or comb his hair until Baldr's killer has been brought "to the funeral pyre". This parallels a comment made by Tacitus in his 1st century work Germania, regarding a Germanic tribe called the Chatti, who may not shave or groom before having first slain an enemy.

In the *Poetic Edda* in *Grímnismál* ('The Lay of Grimnir'), Odin (disguised as Grimnir) describes Vidarr's residence:

"Hrísi vex ok háu grasi
Víðars land viði;
en þar mögr of læzt af mars baki
frækn at hefna föður."

"Brushwood grown and high grass
Vidarr's land of woods;
but there the son leapt from his steed down,
vowing to avenge his father".

In the *Poetic Edda* in *Völuspá* ('The Prophecy of the Völva'), a völva tells Odin that his son Vidarr will avenge Odin's death at *Ragnarök* by stabbing Fenrir in the heart:

"Þá kemr inn mikli
mögr Sigföður,
Víðarr, vega
at valdýri.
Lætr hann megi Hveðrungs
mundum standa
hjör til hjarta,
þá er hefnt föður."

"Then comes the great
son victory-father,
Vidarr, to fight
against the beast.
he abates the son of Hveðrung (Loki)
he-will lay-upon
the sword to the heart
then is avenged the father."

In the *Poetic Edda* in *Vafþrúðnismál* ('The Lay of Vafþrúðnir'), Vafþrúðnir states that after the events of *Ragnarök* ('the Twilight of the Gods'), Vidarr and his brother Vali will both live in the temples of the gods after Surtr's flame has been extinguished, along with the sons of Thor: Modi and Magni.

Later in *Gylfaginning* ('The Beguiling of Gylfi'), Vidarr's battle with Fenrir or the Fenris-wolf is described in more detail.

"Úlfrinn gleypir Óðin. Verðr þat hans bani.

En þegar eftir snýst fram Víðarr ok stígr öðrum fæti í neðra kjöft úlfsins.

Á þeim fæti hefir hann þann skó, er allan aldr hefir verit til samnat.

Þat eru bjórar þeir, er menn sníða ór skóm sínum fyrir tám eða hæli.
Því skal þeim bjórum braut kasta sá maðr, er at því vill hyggja at koma ásunum at liði.

Annarri hendi tekr hann inn efra kjöft úlfsins ok rífr sundr gin hans, ok verðr þat úlfsins bani.
Loki á orrostu við Heimdall, ok verðr hvárr annars bani.
Því næst slyngr Surtr eldi yfir jörðina ok brennir allan heim."

"The Wolf shall swallow Odin; that shall be his ending

But straight thereafter shall Vídarr stride forth and set one foot upon the lower jaw of the Wolf:

on that foot he has the shoe, materials for which have been gathering throughout all time.

(They are the scraps of leather which men cut out: of their shoes at toe or heel;
therefore he who desires in his heart to come to the Æsir's help should cast those scraps away.)

With one hand he shall seize the Wolf's upper jaw and tear his gullet asunder; and that is the death of the Wolf.
Loki shall have battle with Heimdallr, and each be the slayer of the other.
Then straightway shall Surtr cast fire over the earth and burn all the world"

Vidarr stabbing Fenrir while holding his jaws apart by W. G. Collingwood, 1908
Creative Commons, Public Domain

Vili and Ve (Brothers of Odin)

Vili and Ve (Vé ro Véi) are the brothers of Odin, and the sons of Bestla and Borr. Of the three brothers, Odin is the eldest, Vili the middle, and Ve the youngest.

The name Vé in Old Norse means 'sanctuary', and is related to the Gothic weiha ('priest'), the Old English wēoh ('idol'), and Old Saxon wīh ('temple'), all of which come from the Proto-Norse *'*Wiljô'*, and the Proto-Germanic *'*wīhōn'*, *'*wīhą'*, *'*wīhaz'*, and *'*wīhan'* ('holy', 'sanctuary').

The name Vili in Old Norse means 'will', and is related to the Gothic wilja, Old English willa, and Old High Saxon wīh, all of which come from the Proto-Norse *'*Wīhaz'*, and the Proto-Germanic *'*weljōn'* and *'*weljan'* meaning 'will' or 'wish'.

Vili and Ve, together with their brother Odin, are described as the three brothers who slew Ymir, the ancestor of all *jötnar* (giants), which ended the primeval rule of the *jötnar* and began the rule of the *Æsir*.

They are also named in some sources as having created the first humans, Ask and Embla. Odin gave them soul and life, Vili (Hoenir in some sources) gave them wit, intelligence, and touch, and Ve (Lodurr in some sources) gave them countenance, appearance, facial expression, blood, circulation, speech, hearing, and sight.

Chapter 3 of *Heimskringla* says that Odin had two brothers, Vili and Ve. While Odin was gone, his brothers governed his realm. Once Odin was gone for so long that the *Æsir* believed that he would not return, his brothers began to divide up Odin's inheritance, but his wife Frigg they shared between them. However, afterwards, he returned and took possession of his wife again.

02 The Ásynjur

Bil and Hjuki (The Followers of the Moon)

Bil and Hjuki are a sister and brother who follow Mani (the personification of the moon) across the heavens. The name Bil is believed to mean 'instant', and the name Hjuki possibly means 'the one returning to health'.

Scholars discuss and debate their nature, arguing in favour of their role as potential personifications of the craters on the Moon or its phases, and their relation to later folklore in Germanic Europe. Bil has been identified with '*Bilwis*', an agriculture-associated figure that is frequently attested in the folklore of German-speaking areas of Europe.

Bil and Hjuki are mentioned in the *Prose Edda* in *Gylfaginning* ('The Beguiling of Gylfi') as the son and daughter of *Viðfinnr* ('wood-finn').

They were fetching water from the well called *Byrgir* ('hider of something'), carrying a pole on their shoulders called *Simul*, and a pail called *Saeg*, when Mani took them from the earth and into the heavens where they now follow him.

"*Máni stýrir göngu tungls ok ræðr nýjum ok niðum. Hann tók tvau börn af jörðunni, er svá heita, Bil ok Hjúki, er þau gengu frá brunni þeim er, Byrgir heitir, ok báru á öxlum sér sá, er heitir Sægr, en stöngin Simul. Viðfinnr er nefndr faðir þeira. Þessi börn fylgja Mána, svá sem sjá má af jörðu.*"

"Mani steers the course of the moon, and determines its waxing and waning. He took two children from the earth, who are named Bil and Hjuki, as they went from the spring that is named Byrgr, and the bore a pole which is named Saeg, and the pole Simul. Vidfinn is their father named. The children follow Mani, so as seen may be from earth."

A 19th century drawing of The Man in the Moon by L. Richter, 1890
Creative Commons, Public Domain

Eir (Goddess of Healing, the Healing Arts, and Medical Skill)

Eir is a member of the *Æsir*. Her name in Old Norse variously translates as 'protection', 'help', and 'mercy'.

Eir is mentioned in the *Poetic Edda* in *Fjölsvinnsmál* ('The Lay of Fjölsvinn'). She is one of the nine maidens who sit at Menglod's knees on *Lyfjaberg* ('healing-hill' or 'healing-mountain'), a magical place with healing properties. These nine maidens protect those who give offerings or sacrifices to them.

Svipdagr	"...Hvat þat bjarg heitir, er ek sé brúði á þjóðmæra þruma?"	"...What is that mountain called, where I see a bride so splendid standing?"
Fjölsviðr	"Lyfjaberg þat heitir, en þat hefir lengi verit sjúkum ok sárum gaman; heil verðr hver, þótt hafi árs sótt, ef þat klífr, kona."	"Lyfjaberg it is called, and it has long been to the sick and sore good; healed become those who, though have a year's sickness, if a woman climbs it."
Svipdagr	"...Hvat þær meyjar heita, er fyr Menglaðar knjám sitja sáttar saman?"	"...What are those maidens called, who before Menglod's knees sit happily together?"
Fjölsviðr	"Hlíf heitir, önnur Hlífþrasa, þriðja Þjóðvarta, Björt ok Blíð, Blíðr, Fríð, Eir ok Aurboða."	"Hlif one is called, another Hlifthrasa, the third Thjodvarta, Bjort and Blid, Blidr, Frid, Eir and Aurboda."
Svipdagr	"...Hvárt þær bjarga, þeim er blóta þær, ef gerask þarfar þess?"	"...Where are those saved, they who sacrifice to them, if it happens that they have need of this?"

Fjölsviðr	*"Bjarga svinnar, hvar er menn blóta þær á stallhelgum stað; eigi svá hátt forað kemr at hölða sonum, hvern þær ór nauðum nema."*	"Saved are some, who those people sacrifice there at the altars-holy; not so great danger shall come to sons of men, who then out of need shall be saved."

Eir is mentioned in the *Prose Edda* in *Gylfaginning* ('The Beguiling of Gylfi') as one of the *Ásynjur* (the female goddesses of the *Æsir* family of gods). She is described as "the best physician".

Eir is also mentioned in the *Prose Edda* in *Skáldskaparmál* ('The Language of Poetry'), in a subsection called *Nafnaþulur* ('Name-Rhapsody'). *Nafnaþulur* does not appear in every manuscript version of the *Prose Edda* that has been handed down to us through history, and it may be a later addition to Snorri Sturluson's original composition, or one of its sources. The poem lists the names of all of the figures in Norse Mythology by category (e.g: sea kings, giants, troll-wives, sons of Odin, members of the *Æsir*, etc.). Confusingly, Eir's name appears in the list of *Valkyries* (female figures who guide souls of the dead to Odin's hall Valhalla), and not in the list of *Ásynjur* as might be expected. This has led to some speculation among scholars as to whether the various sources compiled in the *Prose Edda* are referring to the same Eir, or whether her role in Norse mythology changed over time.

Valkyrjur. *"26. Enn eru aðrar* *Óðins meyjar:* *Hildr ok Göndul,* *Hlökk, Mist, Skögul,* *þá er Hrund ok Eir,* *Hrist, Skuld talið.* *Nornir heita,* *þær er nauð skapa,* *Nift ok Dísi* *nú mun ek telja."*	Valkyries "26. And these others are Odin's maidens: Hildr and Gondul, Hlokk, Mist, Skogul, then are Hrund and Eir, Hrist, and Skuld listed. Norns are named, those who necessity shape, Nift and Disi I will now name."

An illustration of Menglöð surrounded by nine maidens by Lorenz Frølich, 1895
Creative Commons, Public Domain

Frigg (Goddess of Marriage, Prophecy, and Motherhood)

Frigg is a member of the *Æsir*. In Old High German she is known as '*Frīja*', in Langobardic as '*Frēa*', in Old English as '*Frīg*', in Old Frisian as '*Frīa*', and in Old Saxon as '*Frī*', all of which come from the Proto-Germanic '**Frijjō*'.

Frigg is the daughter of Fjörgynn (the personification of the earth), the wife of Odin (both of whom have the gift of prophecy), and the mother of Baldr. Frigg dwells in a place called *Fensalir* ('fen-halls'), which is said to be very splendid.

Some sources mention that Frigg has a sister called Fulla (Volla, Folla), whose name is translated as 'bountiful'. Fulla carries Frigg's ashen box, looks after her footwear, and shares her secrets.

The goddess Lofn is given special permission by Frigg and Odin to arrange unions among men and women.

The goddess Hlin is instructed by Frigg to protect those that Frigg deems worthy of keeping from danger; and the goddess Gna is sent by Frigg into various worlds to carry out her business.

The modern English weekday name Friday comes from Old English '*Frīgedæġ*' ('Frigg's Day'), comparable with Old Frisian '*Frīadei*', Middle Dutch '*Vridach*', Middle Low German '*Vrīdach*', and Old High German '*Frîatac*'. The Old Norse '*Frjádagr*' was borrowed from a West Germanic language. All of these terms come from the Late Proto-Germanic '**Frijjōdag*'.

Frigg is mentioned in the *Poetic Edda* in *Völuspá* ('The Prophecy of the Völva'), firstly as having wept at the death of her son Baldr, secondly when Odin is referred to as the beloved of Frigg, and thirdly when the death of Odin is foretold and described as Frigg's second grief (the first being her grief at the death of Baldr).

In the *Poetic Edda* in *Lokasenna* ('Loki's Verbal Duel'), Frigg attends a feast hosted by Ægir (giant and god of the sea). Loki insults the gods and accuses Frigg of lustful moral impropriety.

In the *Poetic Edda* in *Vafþrúðnismál* ('The Lay of Vafþrúðnir'), Odin asks the advice of Frigg as to whether it would be wise to seek out the hall of Vafþrúðnir to compete with the all-wise *jötunn* (giant) in a contest of knowledge. Frigg advises Odin against the idea, but Odin nevertheless continues with his quest, ultimately outwitting Vafþrúðnir.

In the *Prose Edda* in *Gylfaginning* ('The Beguiling of Gylfi'), Baldr has a series of nightmares that he will be killed. Taking these dreams seriously as a prophecy, the gods hold a council to discuss Baldr's dreams.

Baldr's mother Frigg, who has also had the same dream of Baldr's death, commands all things across the Nine Realms to promise not to hurt Baldr, but the mistletoe does not make the promise. Frigg is unconcerned by this, as she does not believe it is of any importance.

The gods then amuse themselves by hurling objects at Baldr and watching them bounce off him, causing him no harm at all.

Loki learns of what has happened by disguising himself as a woman and asking Frigg what the *Æsir* are up to at their assembly. He then makes a spear (in some accounts an arrow) out of the mistletoe. Loki then tricks Hodr into throwing the spear (or firing the arrow) of mistletoe and inadvertently killing Baldr, his own brother.

The gods are speechless and devastated by Baldr's death. Frigg asks the *Æsir* who among them wishes to "gain all of her love and favour" by riding the road to Hel. Whoever agrees is to offer Hel a ransom in exchange for Baldr's return to Asgard. Hermodr volunteers to make the journey and sets off on Odin's grey eight-legged horse Sleipnir ('slippy-one').

Hermodr rides to the realm of Hel and speaks to Hel herself, begging for Baldr's release. Hel says that Baldr would only be released if all things, dead and alive, wept for him. All do except for a giantess named Thokk (believed to be Loki in disguise), and so Baldr has to remain in the underworld.

Due to several similarities between Frigg and Freyja, some scholars have proposed that they both descend from a single common Proto-Germanic goddess.

An illustration of Frigg and Odin, sitting in *Hliðskjálf* ('the high seat with the wide view') and gazing into all worlds, by Lorenz Frølich, 1895
Creative Commons, Public Domain

Fulla (Goddess of Plenty, Wealth, and Abundance)

Fulla (Volla, Folla) is a member of the *Æsir*. She is the sister of Frigg, and also her servant maid and messenger.

The name Fulla in Old Norse translates as ('bountiful') from the adjective '*fullr*', comparable with the Gothic '*fullo*' ('fullness') from the adjective '*fulls*', Old High German '*folla*' ('plenitude') from the adjective '*foll*'. All of which comes from the Proto-Germanic '**fullōn*' ('fullness', 'plenitude') from the adjective '**fullaz*'.

In the *Prose Edda* in *Gylfaginning* ('The Beguiling of Gylfi'), Fulla is described wearing a golden headband and tending to Frigg's ashen box and footwear.

"Fimmta er Fulla. Hon er enn mær ok ferr laushár ok gullband um höfuð. Hon berr eski Friggjar ok gætir skóklæða hennar ok veit launráð með henni."

"Fifth is Fulla. She is a maid and goes about with loose hair and a golden band about her head. She carries the ashen box of Frigg and takes care of footwear hers and knows secrets with her."

Also in *Gylfaginning*, after the death of Baldr and his wife Nanna, Hermod petitions Hel for their release. Before Hermod returns, Baldr gives him the ring called *Draupnir* ('the-dripper') for Odin, Nanna gives Hermod a linen robe for Frigg, and a finger ring for Fulla.

In the *Prose Edda* in *Skáldskaparmál* ('The Language of Poetry'), one of the poetic names for gold is given as 'Fulla's Snood'.

In one of the two Merseburg Charms known as 'the Horse Cure', written in 10th century Old High German, *Phol* (Baldr) and *Wodan* (Odin) ride into a wood and discover one of Baldr's young horses has sprained its foot. Fulla is one of the gods that sings charms in order to heal the horse.

"Phol ende uuodan uuorun zi holza.
du uuart demo balderes uolon sin uuoz birenkit.
thu biguol en sinthgunt, sunna era suister;
thu biguol en friia, uolla era suister;
thu biguol en uuodan, so he uuola conda:
sose benrenki, sose bluotrenki, sose lidirenki:
ben zi bena, bluot zi bluoda,
lid zi geliden, sose gelimida sin.

"Phol and Wodan were riding to the woods, and the foot of Balder's foal was sprained
So Sinthgunt, Sunna's sister, conjured it;
and Frija, Volla's sister, conjured it;
and Wodan conjured it, as well he could:
Like bone-sprain, so blood-sprain, so joint-sprain:
Bone to bone, blood to blood,
joints to joints, so may they be glued.

One theory suggests that Fulla, along with Gefjon, Gerdr, and Skadi were all aspects of a single Great Goddess.

Gefjon (Goddess of Ploughing, Foreknowledge, and Chastity)

Gefjon (Gefjun, Gefion) is a member of the *Æsir*. She is associated with the Danish island of Zealand (Sjælland), the legendary Swedish king Gylfi, and the legendary Danish king Skjoldr.

The meaning of her name has been a matter of dispute among scholars, some of which identify Gefjon as an aspect of Freyja or Frigg. The element *Gef-* likely means 'the giving one'.

Another theory is that the name Gefjon comes from the Old Norse '*geð fiá*' meaning 'chaste', hence her association with chastity and virginity.

In the *Poetic Edda* in *Lokasenna* ('Loki's Verbal Duel'), Loki accuses Gefjon of sleeping with a white youth in return for a necklace.

Odin interjects saying that Loki must be mad to rouse Gefjon to anger, as she knows the fates of all men just as Odin himself does.

The white youth that Gefjon is accused of sleeping with may refer to the god Heimdall, as he is described as "the whitest of gods".

Gefjun kvað:
19. "Hví it Æsir tveir skuluð inni hérv sáryrðum sakask?
Loftki þat veit, at hann leikinn er
ok hann fjörg öll fíá."

Loki kvað:
20. "Þegi þú, Gefjun, þess mun ek nú geta,
er þik glapði at geði sveinn inn hvíti,
er þér sigli gaf ok þú lagðir lær yfir."

Óðinn kvað:
21. "Ærr ertu, Loki, ok örviti,
er þú fær þér Gefjun at gremi,
því at aldar örlög
hygg ek, at hon öll of viti
jafngörla sem ek."

Gefjun spoke:
19. "Why the *Æsir* in twain should be, with insults and accusations?
Loki is known that he is a trickster,
And the dwellers in the heavens he hates."

Loki spoke:
20. "Be silent, Gefjun! for now shall I say,
When you beguiled to like the white youth,
who to you gave a necklace, and you laid your thigh over."

Othin spoke:
21. "Mad are you, Loki, and little-knowing,
that you get Gefjun to resentment,
because the fate of all ages
think I, that she all of knows
equally as I do."

Gefjon is mentioned in the *Prose Edda* in *Gylfaginning* ('The Beguiling of Gylfi'), which begins with an account of King Gylfi, who was once the ruler of "what is now called Sweden". King Gylfi gives "a certain vagrant woman, as reward for his entertainment, one plough-land in his kingdom, as much as four oxen could plow up in a day and night". This woman is "of the race of the *Æsir*" and her name is Gefjon.

Gefjon takes four oxen from Jötunheimr ('Realm of the Giants' literally 'Giant-Home') in the north. The four oxen are her sons from a *jötunn* (giant) whose name is not known. Gefjon's plough cuts so hard and deep that it uproots the land. The oxen draw the land out into the sea to the west and halt in a certain sound. Gefjon places the land there and calls it Zealand. The place where the land was taken from is now a lake (either Lake Mälar or Lake Vänern in Sweden).

The Heimskringla tells the same story, and adds that it is Odin who sends Gefjon "north over the sound to seek for land", Gefjon bears four sons with a *jötunn* (giant) and then *turns them into oxen*. Gefjon then marries the legendary Danish king Skjoldr who is described as a "son of Odin". Gefjon and Skjoldr then live happily ever after on Zealand in a place called *Hleiðr* or *Hleiðargarðr* (Modern Danish: Lejre).

The theme of claiming land by how much of it can be travelled in a limited amount of time is common in folk tales from Northern Europe. This theme is believed to contain echoes of ancient rituals of land taking, like lighting fires around newly taken land to cleanse, purify, and prepare the land for fertility, perhaps in connection with the rituals of a fertility goddess like Gefjon.

Gefjon appears in some Old Norse translations of Roman and Greek mythology as a Norse equivalent of Diana / Artemis, Venus / Aphrodite, Minerva / Athena, and Vesta / Hestia.

Gefjon ploughs the earth in Sweden by Lorenz Frølich, 1882
Creative Commons, Public Domain

Gerdr (Goddess of the Earth)

Gerdr (Gerðr, Gerður, Gerd, Gerda, Gerth) is one of the *Jötnar* (giants).

She is the daughter of Gymir and Aurboda, the sister of Beli ('roarer'), and the wife of the god Freyr.

In both the *Poetic Edda* in *Skírnismál* ('The Lay of Skírnir'), and in the *Prose Edda*, the tale is told that Freyr is sitting on the high seat called *Hlidskjalf* ('the high seat with a wide view') from which he can view into all worlds.

Freyr looks into *Jötunheimr* ('Realm of the Giants', literally 'Giant-Home') and sees Gerdr walking from the hall of her father to a storehouse.

Freyr is struck by her shimmering beauty, immediately falls in love with her and becomes heartsick for her.

"Í Gymis görðum ek ganga sá mér tíða mey; armar lýstu, en af þaðan allt loft ok lögr."

"In Gymir's courts I saw walking what I long for, a maiden; her arms shone light and from there all air and waters."

Freyr asks his servant Skírnir go to Jötunheimr to where Gerdr and her father Gymir live, in order to court Gerdr and obtain the promise of her hand in marriage. Skírnir requests that Freyr give him a horse to ride there, and Freyr's sword in order to protect himself on the journey; a magical sword which fights *jötnar* (giants) by itself if the one wielding it is wise enough.

Skírnir arrives at Gymir's courts making such a noise that the earth trembles and shakes. Gerdr is alarmed at the commotion, but tells her serving maid to invite the man into their hall for some of their famous mead. Gerdr is afraid that the man may be her "brother's slayer".

Gerdr asks Skírnir if he is one of the *Álfar* ('Elves'), the *Æsir*, or the *Vanir*, and asks why he has come alone "over the wild fire" to seek their company. Skírnir responds that he is of none of these, but he has sought their company.

Skírnir offers Gerdr eleven golden apples, representing eternal life, in order to gain her favour. Gerdr rejects the apples no matter who offers them and adds that neither will she and Freyr be together as long as they live. Skírnir offers Gerdr a ring called *Draupnir* ('the-dripper') that produces eight more gold rings every ninth night and "was burned with Odin's young son". Gerdr responds that she is not interested in the ring, for she shares her father's property, and Gymir has no lack of gold.

At Gerdr's rejection, Skírnir then resorts to a series of ever more elaborate threats and curses, from cutting her head from her neck, to imprisonment, public humiliation, madness, unbearable desire, tears of grief, harassment, hopelessness, marriage to an ugly three-headed giant, wasting away in misery, and ultimately bringing down the potent wrath of the gods (these threats however are not mentioned in the *Prose Edda*).

Gerdr gives in and welcomes Skírnir to take a crystal cup of ancient mead, commenting that she never thought she would love one of the *Vanir*. She agrees to meet Freyr in a place called *Barri* (Barrey or Barey, possibly 'barley-island' or 'grain-island', possibly a symbolic meaning linked with fertility).

"Barri heitir,
er vit bæði vitum,
lundr lognfara;
en eft nætr níu
þar mun Njarðar syni
Gerðr unna gamans."

"Barri is named,
that knowledge both we know,
a calm grove;
but after nine nights
there will be Njord's son (Freyr)
Gerdr will grant delight."

The meeting place of Gerdr and Freyr is also mentioned in the *Prose Edda* in *Gylfaginning* ('The Beguiling of Gylfi'):

"ok níu nóttum síðar skyldi hon þar koma, er Barrey heitir, ok ganga þá at brullaupinu með Frey."

"and nine nights after should she there come, to where Barrey is named, and go then to the wedding-feast with Freyr."

Skírnir rides home to find Freyr standing outside. Freyr immediately greets Skírnir and asks for news. Skírnir tells him that Gerdr says she will meet with him at Barri. Freyr, impatient and heartsick for Gerdr, comments that one night is long, as is two nights, and questions how he will bear three, noting that frequently a month seems shorter than half a night waiting to be with Gerdr.

According to legend, Gerdr and Freyr give birth to a son named Fjolnir who goes on to become the king of Sweden, reigning from Gamla Uppsala (Old Uppsala, Sweden) around the 1st century BCE to the 1st century CE.

Gerdr's brother Beli is indeed slain by Freyr as Gerdr predicted. Freyr is without his sword which he gave to Skírnir, but still manages to kill Beli with the antler of a hart (stag), although he could have killed him with his bare hands.

The resulting dynasty of kings that descend from Gerdr and Freyr's son Fjolnir became known as the *Yngling Dynasty*.

They are also known in Old Norse as 'skilfingar', and in the Old English poem Beowulf as 'scylfings'.

Harald Fairhair, the first king and ruler of all Norway is said to descend from a branch of the *Yngling Dynasty*.

Left: Skyrnir and Gerda by Harry George Theaker, 1920
Creative Commons, Public Domain

Gna and Hofvarpnir (Messengers of Frigg)

Gna (Gná) is a member of the *Æsir*. She is a goddess who runs errands in other worlds for the goddess Frigg. She is thought by scholars to be a goddess of fullness.

In the Prose Edda in Gylfaginning ('the Beguiling of Gylfi'), King Gylfi (who calles himself Gangleri) engages in a test of wisdom with three men on thrones called Hár ('high'), Jafnhár ('just-as-high'), and Þriði ('the-Third').

Descriptions are given of 16 *Ásynjur* (female goddesses of the *Æsir*). Gna is thirteenth or fourteenth in the list (depending on the source).

Hár mentions that Frigg sends Gna off to different worlds to run errands.

She rides the flying sea-treading horse Hofvarpnir (Hófvarpnir, 'he who throws his hoofs', 'hoof thrower', or 'hoof kicker').

Hofvarpnir has the ability to ride through the air and over the sea, and "once some *Vanir* saw her path as she rode through the air".

"Fjórtánda Gná, hana sendir Frigg í ýmsa heima at erendum sínum.	"The fourteenth is Gná: her Frigg sends into various realms on errands hers;
Hon á þann hest, er renn loft ok lög ok heitir Hófvarpnir.	She has that horse, which runs over sky and sea and is named Hoof-Thrower.
Þat var eitt sinn, er hon reið, at Vanir nökkurir sá reið hennar í loftinu. Þá mælti einn:	It was once, when she was riding, that some of the *Vanir* saw her course in the air. Then one spoke:
"Hvat þar flýgr, *hvat þar ferr* *eða at lofti líðr?"*	What flies there? What fares there, Or glideth in the air?
Hon svarar:	She answered:
"Né ek flýg, *þó ek ferk* *ok at lofti líðk* *á Hófvarpni,* *þeim er Hamskerpir* *gat við Garðrofu."*	"I fly not, though I fare And in the air glide On Hoof-Thrower, him that Hamskerpir begat with Gardrofa."

Hlin (The Protector and Giver of Refuge)

Hlin (Hlín) is a member of the *Æsir* who is one of Frigg's servants. Her name is translated as meaning 'protector', based on the Old Norse '*hlynr*' ('maple tree'), from the Proto-Germanic '**hluniz*' ('maple').

In folklore, maple trees are associated with strength, endurance, and wisdom, often seen as sacred or auspicious. Maple leaves have been used as protective talismans in various cultures, believed to ward off evil spirits and harm. Scholars believe this suggests a wider tradition of protective tree goddesses.

For example, according to *Skáldskaparmál* ('The Language of Poetry'), the rowan tree is called the "salvation of Thor" because Thor once saved himself by clinging to it. It has been theorised that Thor's wife, Sif, once came into being in the form of a rowan tree to which Thor clung.

Also the name of the goddess *Ilmr* is believed to be related to the Old Norse common noun '*almr*' ('elm tree').

In the *Prose Edda* in *Gylfaginning* ('The Beguiling of Gylfi'), Hár describes the goddesses, and the twelfth goddess is Hlín. She is instructed by Frigg to protect those that Frigg deems worthy of keeping from danger. Following her name, a proverb is mentioned whereby someone who escapes finds '*hleinir*', which has been translated as 'refuge' or 'peace and quiet'.

"Tólfta Hlín, hon er sett til gæzlu yfir þeim mönnum,
er Frigg vill forða við háska nökkurum.

Þaðan af er þat orðtak,
at sá, er forðast, hleinir."

"The twelfth is Hlín: she is set to keep-watch over those men,
whom Frigg desires to preserve from any danger;
From-there comes the saying,
that he who escapes finds refuge."

In the *Poetic Edda* poem *Völuspá* ('The Prophecy of the Völva'), Hlin is mentioned in the foretelling of the death of Odin and the immense battle during the events of Ragnarök ('the Twilight of the Gods'), which will cause Hlin and Frigg great sorrow. This sorrow is described as 'another harm', the first being the death of Frigg's son Baldr.

53. Þá kemr Hlínar
harmr annarr fram,
er Óðinn ferr
við ulf vega,
en bani Belja
bjartr at Surti;
þá mun
Friggjar falla angan.

53. Now comes to Hlin
yet another hurt,
When Othin fares
to fight with the wolf,
And Beli's fair slayer
seeks out Surt,
For there must fall
the joy of Frigg.

Idunn (Goddess of Apples and Eternal Youth)

Idunn (Iðunn, Idhunn, Idunn, Idun, Ithun, Iduna, Idunna) is a member of the *Æsir*. She is the keeper of the apples of eternal youthfulness, and she is the wife of Bragi.

In the *Prose Edda* in *Skáldskaparmál* ('The Language of Poetry'), Loki is forced by a *jötunn* (giant) named Thjazi to lure Idunn out of *Asgard* and into a wood with the promise of apples even fairer than her own.

Thjazi, in the form of an eagle, abducts Idunn from the wood and carries her home. Idunn's absence causes the gods to grow old and grey, and they realize that Loki is responsible for her disappearance.

Loki is then forced to bring Idunn back, setting out in the form of a falcon, eventually finding her alone at Thjazi's home. He turns her into a nut and flies back toward Asgard with her.

When Thjazi returns home to find Idunn gone, he assumes his eagle form and flies off in pursuit of Loki.

The gods build a pyre in the courtyard of *Asgard*, and just as Loki has stopped short of the fire, the gods kindle the fire further, and Thjazi in eagle form is unable to slow down in time. Thjazi plunges headlong through the fire, falling to the ground with his feathers alight and the gods attack and kill him.

Idunn is also mentioned in the *Poetic Edda* in *Lokasenna* ('Loki's Verbal Duel'). Loki insults Idunn by accusing her of embracing her brother's slayer. The event that Loki is referring to has not survived in sources, but appears to echo a theme of embracing one's brother's slayer, as in the story of Gerdr and her husband Freyr, as Freyr kills Gerdr's brother Beli.

Iðunn kvað:
16. "Bið ek þik, Bragi, barna sifjar duga
ok allra óskmaga, at þú Loka
kveðir-a lastastöfum Ægis höllu í."

Loki kvað:
17. "Þegi þú, Iðunn, þik kveð ek allra kvenna

vergjarnasta vera, síztu arma þína
lagðir ítrþvegna um þinn bróðurbana."

Iðunn kvað:
18. "Loka ek kveðk-a lastastöfum
Ægis höllu í:
Braga ek kyrri bjórreifan;
vilk-at ek, at it vreiðir vegizk."

Idunn spoke:
16. "I ask you, Bragi, child of affinity to support
and of all wishes, that you Loki
speak not vicious words in Ægir's hall."

Loki spoke:
17. "Be you silent, Idunn! to you say I of all women
mad after men, of all your arms
laid full-washed about your brother's slayer."

Idunn spoke:
18. "To Loki I speak not vicious words
in Ægir's hall;
Bragi I calm, cheerful from beer drinking;
I wish not, that it goes the way of anger."

In the poem *Hrafnagaldr Óðins* ('Odin's Raven Chant'), additional information is given about Idunn, though this information does not appear in any other sources. Idunn is identified as descending from elves, as one of "Ivaldi's elder children" and as a *dís* (a female deity, ghost, or spirit associated with fate) who dwells in dales:

"Dvelur í dölum	"Dwelling in dales
dís forvitin,	the foreknowing dís,
Yggdrasils frá	Yggdrasil's from
aski hnigin;	ash descending;
álfa ættar	of elven kin
Iðunni hétu,	Idunni named,
Ívalds eldri	Ívalds eldest
yngsta barna."	younger children."

Idunn is named as Bragi's wife in the *Prose Edda* in *Gylfaginning* ('The Beguiling of Gylfi'):

"Kona hans er Iðunn.	"His wife is Idunn.
Hon varðveitir í eski sínu epli þau, er goðin skulu á bíta, þá er þau eldast,	She preserves in her ash-box those apples, which the gods shall bite, then when they are old,
ok verða þá allir ungir,	and they become all younger,
ok svá mun vera allt til ragnarökrs."	and so shall it be all until *Ragnarök*."

Loki and Idun by John Bauer, 1911
Creative Commons, Public Domain

Lofn (Goddess of Marriage and Union)

Lofn is a member of the *Æsir*. She is one of Frigg's servants who is given special permission by Frigg and Odin to arrange unions among men and women, even if they have been forbidden or banned.

Her name in Old Norse possibly means 'the comforter', 'the comforting one', 'mild', 'the mild one', 'loving', or 'the loving one'.

In the *Prose Edda* in *Gylfaginning* ('The Beguiling of Gylfi'), descriptions are given of 16 *Ásynjur* (goddesses of the *Æsir*). Lofn is the eighth in the list:

"Átta Lofn, hon er svá mild ok góð til áheita,	"The eighth is Lofn, she is so mild and good to call upon,
at hon fær leyfi af Alföðr eða Frigg til manna samgangs,	that she has leave from the Allfather (Odin) or Frigg for the coming together of mankind,
kvinna ok karla, þótt áðr sé bannat eða þvertekit þykki.	women and men, though it was forbidden or thought denied.
Þat er af hennar nafni lof kallat ok svá þat, at hon er lofuð mjök af mönnum."	It is from her the name 'praise' is called and so it is, that she is loved much by people".

In the *Prose Edda* in *Skáldskaparmál* ('The Language of Poetry'), Lofn is included among a list of 27 *Ásynjur*, and elsewhere her name appears as a poetic term or kenning for 'woman'.

Scholars have followed Snorri Sturluson's connection with the name Lofn and the word lof- meaning 'praise'. Some scholars theorise that Lofn may be another name for Frigg, or one of several aspects of Frigg.

Nanna (Wife of Baldr)

Nanna is a goddess associated with the god Baldr. She is the daughter of Nepr, and the wife of Baldr, and the mother of Forseti. The meaning of her name in Old Norse is debated, and theories range from 'mother', 'the daring one', and 'she who empowers'.

The gods are speechless and devastated by the death of Nana's husband Baldr. Beings from all of the Nine Realms attend his funeral. When Nanna sees Baldr's corpse being carried to his ship *Hringhorni* to be burnt, she collapses and dies from her grief. She is then placed on Baldr's ship and the two are set aflame and pushed out to sea. They are then reunited in Hel.

In the *Prose Edda* in *Gylfaginning* ('The Beguiling of Gylfi'), after Baldr's funeral and at the request of Frigg, Hermodr rides to the realm of Hel. When he reaches Hel's hall, he sees Baldr seated in the most honourable seat, and he then stays the night. The next morning, Hermodr begs Hel to release Baldr to return to Asgard, recounting the great sorrow and weeping that his death has caused the Æsir. Hel announces that Baldr will only be released if all things, whether dead or alive, weep for him.

Before Hermodr returns to *Asgard* with Hel's message, Baldr gives Hermodr the ring *Draupnir* ('the-dripper') which had been burned with him on his funeral pyre, to take back to Odin. Nanna gives Hermodr a linen robe for Frigg along with other gifts, and a finger-ring for Fulla.

> "Þá stóð Hermóðr upp, en Baldr leiddi hann út ór höllinni ok tók hringinn Draupni ok sendi Óðni til minja, en Nanna sendi Frigg rifti ok enn fleiri gjafar. Fullu fingrgull."

> "Then Hermodr arose; but Baldr led him out of the hall, and took the ring Draupnir and sent it to Odin for remembrance. And Nanna sent Frigg a linen robe, and yet more gifts, and to Fulla a golden finger-ring."

Njorun (Mysterious Goddess of the Earth)

Njorun (Njǫrun, Njörun) is a mysterious goddess about whom little is known. Scholars debate the connection of the name Njorun to that of the god Njord, possibly as a divine pairing of gods whose names are smiliar and represent masculine and feminine aspects of the divine, and possibly coming from the same root of an older god named Nerthus (from the Proto-Germanic '*Nerþuz'). It could be that Njorun is in fact the unnamed 'Sister-Wife of Njord'.

Njorun is also mentioned in the *Prose Edda* in *Skáldskaparmál* ('The Language of Poetry'), in a subsection called *Nafnaþulur* ('Name-Rhapsody'). *Nafnaþulur* does not appear in every manuscript version of the *Prose Edda* that has been handed down to us through history, and it may be a later addition to Snorri Sturluson's original composition, or one of its sources. The poem lists the names of all of the figures in Norse Mythology by category (e.g: sea kings, giants, troll-wives, sons of Odin, members of the *Æsir*, etc.). Njorun appears with the *Ásynjur*.

*23. Now shall the goddesses
all be named:
Frigg and Freyja,
Fulla and Snotra,
Gerðr and Gefjon,
Gná, Lofn, Skaði,
Jörð and Iðunn,
Ilmr,1 Bil, Njörun.*

*23. Nú skal Ásynjur
allar nefna:
Frigg ok Freyja,
Fulla ok Snotra,
Gerðr ok Gefjon,
Gná, Lofn, Skaði,
Jörð ok Iðunn,
Ilmr, Bil, Njörun.*

The name Njorun also appears as part of several poetic terms or kennings for women, such as *Eld-Njörun* ('Fire-Njorun'), and *Draum-Njörun* ('Dream-Njorun').

Ran (Goddess of the Sea)

Ran (Rán) is a member of the *Æsir*. She is the personification of the sea, and the wife of the *jötunn* (giant) Ægir (who is also a personification of the sea).

She is the mother of the Nine Sisters (also known as the Nine Mothers of Heimdall).

She is frequently associated with a net which she uses to capture seafarers.

Her name in Old Norse means 'plundering', 'theft', or 'robbery', perhaps signifying her taking of seafarers, for which people would have prayed to her in order to appease her and be spared of her net. The true meaning of her name however has not been fully clarified.

Ran is seen as the sinister side of the sea who rules the realm of the dead at the bottom of the sea where all those who have drowned go, whereas her husband Ægir personifies the sea as a friendly power.

Poets or skalds use her name in kennings when referring to the sea, for example *Ránar-land* ('Ran's land'), *Ránar-salr* ('Ran's hall'), and *Ránar-vegr* ('Ran's way'), and *rán-beðr* ('the bed of Ran') and meaning the bed of the sea. Also the phrase to 'give someone to Ran' means to drown them.

According to the *Poetic Edda*, the Völsunga saga, and *Reginsmál* ('The Lay of Reginn'), Ran once loaned her net to Loki so that he could catch Andvari, a dwarf who lives underneath a waterfall who has the power to change himself into a pike at will.

"Þá sendu þeir Loka at afla gullsins. Hann kom til Ránar ok fekk net hennar ok fór þá til Andvarafors ok kastaði netinu fyrir gedduna, en hon hljóp í netit."	"Then they sent Loki to get the gold. He came to Ran and got her net and went then to Andvari's fall and cast the net in front of the pike, and it jumped into the net."

The 10th century poet, sorcerer, berserker, and farmer Egill Skallagrímsson (the anti-hero of Egil's Saga) laments the death of his son Bodvar, who drowned at sea during a storm:

Mjök hefr Rán rykst um mik;	Greatly has Ran afflicted about me;
emk ofsnauðr at ástvinum.	I have been robbed of a great friend.
Sleit marr bönd mínnar áttar,	Broken in the sea bound my descendent,
snaran þátt af sjalfum mér.	Snared is of myself from me.

Later in the poem Egil imagines taking revenge on Ægir and Ran with his sword:

Veiztu um þá sǫk	Know-you about that offence
sverði of rækak,	Sword of swearing
var ǫlsmiðr	Would be the ale-smith (Ægir)

allra tíma;	Of all time;
hroða vágs brœðr	Roughly indented brother
ef vega mættak;	If we met;
fœra ek andvígr	Would I bring onslaught
Ægis mani.	To Ægir's wife (Ran).

In the legendary Frithiof's Saga (*Friðþjófs saga hins frœkna*), Frithiof (*Friðþjófr*) and his men find themselves in a violent storm, and the protagonist mourns that he will soon rest in Ran's bed:

"Sat ek á bólstri	"On a bolster I sit
í Baldrshaga,	in Baldr's mead,
kvað, hvat ek kunna,	speaking, what I know,
fyr konungs dóttur.	before the king's daughter.
Nú skal ek Ránar	Now shall I Ran's
raunbeð troða,	sea-bed tread,
en annar mun	and another shall-be
Ingibjargar."	by Ingibjorg's side."

Rán pulls her net beside her husband Ægir by Friedrich Wilhelm Heine, 1882
Creative Commons, Public Domain

Rindr (Mother of Vali, The Divine Avenger)

Rindr (Rinda, Rind) is a member of the *Æsir*. She is variously described as a *jötunn* (giant), a goddess, or a human princess. She is the mother of Váli, who was fathered by Odin. Vali was born for the sole purpose of avenging Baldr's death. He grew to full adulthood within one day of his birth, and slew Hodr as punishment for killing his own brother. The event is foretold in Baldrs draumar (Baldr's Dreams'):

"Rindr ber Vála
í vestrsölum,
sá mun Óðins sonr
einnættr vega:
hönd of þvær
né höfuð kembir,
áðr á bál of berr
Baldrs andskota;
nauðug sagðak,
nú mun ek þegja."

"Rindr shall bear Vali
In the western halls,
And so shall Odin's son
After one night slay:
Hand of theirs
Not head shall comb
Before to the pyre of bearing
Baldr's enemy;
Forced I spoke,
Now should I be silent."

This is also referred to in *Skáldskaparmál* ('The Language of Poetry'):

"Hvernig skal kenna Vála? Svá, at kalla hann son Óðins ok Rindar, stjúpson Friggjar, bróður ásanna, hefniás Baldrs, dólg Haðar ok bana hans, byggvanda föðurtófta."

"How shall be known Vali? So, that call him son Odin's and Rindr, stepson of Frigg, brother of the *Æsir*, avenger of Baldr, foe of Hodr and his slayer, dweller in the fathers homesteads."

Saga (The Seeress)

Saga (Sága) is a goddess associated with the location *Sokkvabekkr* (Sökkvabekkr, 'sunken bank', 'sunken bench', or 'treasure bank'). *Sokkvabekkr* is believed to be connected to Frigg's residence *Fensalir* ('Fen Halls').

The name Saga is generally thought to be connected to the Old Norse verb '*sjá*', meaning 'to see' (from Proto-Germanic '*sehwan*'). This suggests that Saga is a seeress, and it is possible that Saga may also be a nickname or epithet for an aspect of Frigg representing her gift of prophecy.

*7. Sökkvabekkr heitir inn fjórði,
en þar svalar knegu unnir yfir glymja;
þar þau Óðinn ok Sága drekka um alla daga,
glöð ór gullnum kerum.*

7. Sokkvabekk is named the fourth,
But there could the waves over flow;
There where Odin and Saga drink about all the Day, happily with golden cups.

In the Old Norse poem *Helgakviða Hundingsbana I* ('The First Lay of Helgi Hundingsbane', also known as *Völsungakviða*), Saga is mentioned in an exchange of insults between Helgi and his half-brother Sinfjotli. The location is translated as 'Saga's Headland' which is a reference to *Sokkvabekkr*. However, part of this stanza is missing.

In the *Prose Edda* in *Gylfaginning* ('The Beguiling of Gylfi'), Hár describes the *Ásynjur*, Frigg, and her dwelling:

*"Önnur er Sága.
Hon býr á Sökkvabekk,
ok er þat mikill staðr."*

"Another (second) is Saga:
She dwells at Sokkvabekk,
and that is a great abode."

Sif (Goddess of Fertility, Family, and Wedlock)

Sif is a member of the *Æsir*. She is the wife of Thor and the mother of Ullr, Modi, Magni, and Thrudr. She is a goddess of fertility, family, wedlock, and rowan trees. Sif is described as a golden-haired goddess, perhaps representing fields of golden wheat.

According to *Skáldskaparmál* ('The Language of Poetry'), the rowan tree is called the "salvation of Thor" because Thor once saved himself by clinging to it. It has been theorised that Sif once came into being in the form of a rowan tree to which Thor clung.

Sif has been compared to the Saami goddess *Ravdna*. The red berries of the rowan tree are sacred to *Ravdna*, which is similar to the North Germanic words for the rowan tree: '*reynir*'. *Ravdna* is also the wife of the Saami thunder god *Horagalles* or *Thora Galles*, an equivalent to Thor. These similarities suggest contact between the Saami and seafaring Norsemen across Norway, Sweden, Finland, and the Kola Peninsula in Russia.

In the Prologue of the *Prose Edda*, Snorri states that Thor married Sif, and that she is known as "a prophetess called Sibyl, though we know her as Sif". Snorri also mentions that they produced a son by the name of Loridi.

Perhaps the worst insult that can be uttered against a goddess who represents wedlock and fidelity is the accusation of infidelity. Such accusations appear in at least two sources.

In the *Poetic Edda* in *Hárbarðsljóð* ('The Lay of Harbardr'), Harbardr and Thor engage in an exchange of insults when Harbardr refuses to carry Thor across a swollen river. Harbardr insults Thor by implying that Sif has a lover at home.

Hárbarðr kvað: *48. "Sif á hó heima,* *hans muntu fund vilja,* *þann muntu þrek drýgja,* *þat er þér skyldara."*	Harbardr spoke: 48. "Sif has a lover at home, him should you wish to find, you shall of strength commit, that is your urgent-business."
Þórr kvað: *49. "Mælir þú at munns ráði,* *svá at mér skyldi verst þykkja,* *halr inn hugblauði,* *hygg ek, at þú ljúgir."*	Thor spoke: 49. "Speak you that which should determine, so that to me should the worst seem, a man cowardly, think I, that you are lying."

In the poem *Lokasenna* ('Loki's Verbal Duel'), Loki insults Sif by suggesting that she has had an affair with him. Sif does not respond to this insult, and the exchange of insults turns to Beyla, one of Freyr's servants.

þá gekk Sif fram ok byrlaði Loka í hrímkálki mjöð ok mælti: *53. "Heill ver þú nú, Loki, ok tak við hrímkálki* *fullum forns mjaðar, heldr þú hana eina* *látir með ása sonum vammalausa vera."*	Then went Sif from and poured Loki a cup of mead and spoke: 53. "Hailed be you now, Loki, and take with this cup full of ancient mead, rather you alone set with the Æsir's sons faultless being."
Hann tók við horni ok drakk af: *54. "Ein þú værir, ef þú svá værir,* *vör ok gröm at veri;* *einn ek veit, svá at ek vita þykkjumk,* *hór ok af Hlórriða,* *ok var þat sá inn lævísi Loki."*	He took with the horn and drank of: 54. "Alone you were, if you so shelter, shunned and grudging to be; alone I know, so that I know thinking, adultery and from the arms of Loridi (the son of Thor), and was it so, the cunning Loki."

Sif by John Charles Dollman, 1909
Creative Commons, Public Domain

Sigyn (Wife of Loki)

Loki and Sigyn by Mårten Eskil Winge, 1863
Creative Commons, Public Domain

Sigyn is a member of the Æsir. She is the wife of Loki and the mother of Nari or Narfi and Vali. Her name in Old Norse means 'woman of victory' or 'a friend of victory'.

Little is known about her other than her role in helping Loki while he is being punished for the death of Baldr.

In the *Poetic Edda* in *Völuspá* ('The Prophecy of the Völva'), the völva (seeress) sees Sigyn sitting unhappily with her bound husband Loki under a "grove of hot springs".

35. "Haft sá hon liggja und Hveralundi, lægjarns líki Loka ápekkjan; þar sitr Sigyn þeygi of sínum ver vel glýjuð. Vituð ér enn - eða hvat?"

35. "She has seen lying under hot spring groves, humbled body Loki similar to; there sits Sigyn though not glad or well gleeful. Do you understand, or what?"

In the *Poetic Edda* in *Lokasenna*, Sigyn assists Loki by collecting drips of venom in a shell that would otherwise drip into Loki's eyes:

"En eftir þetta falst Loki í Fránangrsforsi í lax líki. Þar tóku Æsir hann. Hann var bundinn með þörmum sonar síns, Vála, en Narfi, sonr hans, varð at vargi.

"And after that hid Loki in Franang's waterfall like a salmon, there the gods took him. He was bound with the bowels of his son Vali, but Narfi, his son, was changed to a wolf.

Skaði tók eitrorm ok festi upp yfir annlit Loka. Draup þar ór eitr.

Skadi took a poison-snake and fastened it up over Loki's face, the poison dropped thereon.

Sigyn, kona Loka, sat þar ok helt munnlaug undir eitrið. En er munnlaugin var full, bar hon út eitrið, en meðan draup eitrit á Loka.

Sigyn, Loki's wife, sat there and held a shell under the poison, but when the shell was full she carried away the poison, and meanwhile the poison dropped on Loki.

Þá kippðist hann svá hart við, at þaðan af skalf jörð öll. Þat eru nú kallaðir landsskjálftar."

Then he struggled so hard, then the whole earth shook; That is now called an earthquake"

Sigyn is also mentioned in the *Prose Edda* in *Skáldskaparmál* ('The Language of Poetry'), in a subsection called *Nafnaþulur* ('Name-Rhapsody'), in the section called *Ásynjur* (Goddesses).

24. "Hlín ok Nanna, Hnoss, Rindr ok Sjöfn, Sól ok Sága, Sigyn ok Vör. Þá er Vár, ok Syn verðr at nefna, en Þrúðr ok Rán þeim næst talið."

24. "Hlin and Nanna, Hnoss, Rindr and Sjofn, Sol and Saga, Sigyn and Vor. There is Var, and Syn needs to be named, and Thrudr and Ran are named next after them."

Sjofn (Goddess of Love)

Sjofn (Sjǫfn, Sjöfn) is a goddess associated with love. In the *Prose Edda* in *Gylfaginning* ('The Beguiling of Gylfi'), Hár lists the goddesses, and Sjofn is seventh on the list.

"Sjaunda Sjöfn, hon gætir mjök til at snúa hugum manna til ásta, kvinna ok karla, ok af hennar nafni er elskhuginn kallaðr sjafni."

"The seventh is Sjofn: she is most diligent in turning the thoughts of men to love, both of women and of men; and from her name love-longing is called sjafni."

Sjofn is also mentioned in the *Prose Edda* in *Skáldskaparmál* ('The Language of Poetry'), in a subsection called *Nafnaþulur* ('Name-Rhapsody'). *Nafnaþulur* does not appear in every manuscript version of the *Prose Edda* that has been handed down to us through history, and it may be a later addition to Snorri Sturluson's original composition, or one of its sources.

The poem lists the names of all of the figures in Norse Mythology by category (e.g: sea kings, giants, troll-wives, sons of Odin, members of the *Æsir*, etc.).

24. "Hlín ok Nanna,
Hnoss, Rindr ok Sjöfn,
Sól ok Sága,
Sigyn ok Vör.
Þá er Vár, ok Syn
verðr at nefna,
en Þrúðr ok Rán
þeim næst talið."

24. "Hlin and Nanna,
Hnoss, Rindr and Sjöfn,
Sol and Saga,
Sigyn and Vor.
There is Var, and Syn
becomes to be named,
and Thrudr and Ran
are numbered next after them."

Skadi (Goddess of Winter and Mountains)

Skadi (Skaði, Skade, Skathi) is a member of the *Vanir*. She is a goddess of bowhunting, skiing, winter, and mountains.

She is the daughter of the *jötunn* (giant) Thjazi, and she was once married to Njord.

She is also referred to as Ondurgud (ski God) and Ondurdis (Ski-dis, 'dis' being a spirit of fate).

Skadi's marriage to Njord was part of the compensation given by the gods for having killed her father Thjazi.

Skadi provides them with her terms of settlement, and the gods agree that Skadi may choose a husband from among themselves. However, Skadi must choose this husband by looking solely at their feet. Skadi saw a pair of feet that she found particularly attractive and said "I choose that one; there can be little that is ugly about Baldr." However, the owner of the feet turned out to be Njord.

Skadi also included in her terms of settlement that the gods must do something she thought impossible for them to do: make her laugh. To do so, Loki tied one end of a cord around the beard of a nanny goat and the other end around his testicles. The goat and Loki drew one another back and forth, both squealing loudly. Loki dropped into Skadi's lap, and Skadi laughed, completing this part of the atonement. Finally, in compensation to Skadi, Odin took Thjazi's eyes, launched them into the sky, and from the eyes made two stars.

Skadi and Njord attempt to divide their time between Skadi's home of Thrymheimr and Njord's home Noatun, however they soon discover that they are ill-suited to each other's homes. Njord finds the hills and the wailing of wolves loathsome, and Skadi cannot sleep on the sea beds for the wailing of waterfowl.

In the *Poetic Edda* in *Grímnismál* ('the Lay of Grimnir'), Odin mentions Skadi's home of Thrymheimr as consisting of "ancient courts" and refers to Skadi as "the shining bride of the gods".

Skaði kvað:
11. "Þrymheimr heitir inn sétti, er Þjazi bjó sá inn ámáttki jötunn;, en nú Skaði byggvir, skír brúðr goða, fornar tóftir föður."

11. "Thrymheimr is named the sixth, where Thjazi lived, so the almighty giant; and now Skadi dwells, shining bride of the gods, in the home of her father."

Skadi appears in *Lokasenna* ('Loki's Verbal Duel'), telling Loki that he is soon to be punished for his actions. Loki responds by insulting her, stating that he was present at the death of her father.

Skaði kvað:
49. "Létt er þér, Loki;
mun-at-tu lengi svá leika lausum hala,
því at þik á hjörvi skulu

Skadi spoke:
49. "Light are you, Loki;
should-that-you no longer play with your tail,
because that you to a rock's point,

*ins hrímkalda magar
görnum binda goð."*

with the cold entrails
and guts bound by the gods."

*Loki kvað:
50. "Veiztu, ef mik á hjörvi skulu ins hrímkalda magar
görnum binda goð, fyrstr ok efstr*

var ek at fjörlagi, þars vér á Þjaza þrifum."

Loki spoke:
50. "Know-you, if I to a rock's point with the cold entrails
and guts bound by the gods, first and foremost
it was I at the slaughter, there when we on Thjazi assailed."

Skadi appears during the punishment of Loki for the death of Baldr, holding a giant serpent above Loki's head which drips with venom.

*En eftir þetta falst Loki í Fránangrsforsi í lax líki.
Þar tóku Æsir hann.
Hann var bundinn með þörmum sonar síns, Vála, en Narfi, sonr hans, varð at vargi.*

*Skaði tók eitrorm ok festi upp yfir annlit Loka.
Draup þar ór eitr.
Sigyn, kona Loka, sat þar ok helt munnlaug undir eitrið.
En er munnlaugin var full, bar hon út eitrið, en meðan draup eitrit á Loka.*

*Þá kippðist hann svá hart við, at þaðan af skalf jörð öll.
Þat eru nú kallaðir landsskjálftar.*

And after that hid Loki in Franang's waterfall like a salmon,
there the gods took him.
He was bound with the bowels of his son Vali, but Narfi, his son, was changed to a wolf.

Skadi took a poison-snake and fastened it up over Loki's face,
the poison dropped thereon.
Sigyn, Loki's wife, sat there and held a shell under the poison,
but when the shell was full she carried away the poison, and meanwhile the poison dropped on Loki.

Then he struggled so hard, then the whole earth shook;
That is now called an earthquake

Skadi's longing for the mountains by W G Collingwood, 1908
Creative Commons, Public Domain

Snotra (Goddess of Wisdom)

Snotra is a goddess of wisdom. She is the mother of Gautrek son-of-Gauti, the ancestor of the Geats and the Goths.

The Geats were a large North Germanic tribe who inhabited Götaland ('land of the Geats') in modern southern Sweden from antiquity until the Late Middle Ages.

The Goths, were a Germanic people who played a major role in the fall of the Western Roman Empire and the emergence of Medieval Europe.

Snotra's name comes from the Old Norse word '*snotr*', which means 'wise', 'clever', 'prudent', 'intelligent', 'discerning', or 'sagacious'.

The Old Norse word '*snotr*' is similar to the Old English '*snotor*', Old High German '*snottor*', and Gothic '*snutrs*'. All of these come from the Proto-Germanic '**snutraz*'.

In the *Prose Edda* in *Gylfaginning* ('The Beguiling of Gylfi'), Snotra is listed among the gods and goddesses, and described as "prudent".

"Þrettánda Snotra, hon er vitr ok látprúð. Af hennar heiti er kallat snotr kona eða karlmaðr, sá er hóflátr er."	"Snotra is thirteenth: she is prudent and of gentle bearing; from her name a woman or a man who is moderate is called snotr."

Snotra is also mentioned in the *Prose Edda* in *Skáldskaparmál* ('The Language of Poetry'), in a subsection called *Nafnaþulur* ('Name-Rhapsody'). *Nafnaþulur* does not appear in every manuscript version of the *Prose Edda* that has been handed down to us through history, and it may be a later addition to Snorri Sturluson's original composition, or one of its sources. The poem lists the names of all of the figures in Norse Mythology by category (e.g: sea kings, giants, troll-wives, sons of Odin, members of the Æsir, etc.).

23. "Nú skal *Ásynjur* allar nefna: Frigg ok Freyja, Fulla ok Snotra, Gerðr ok Gefjon, Gná, Lofn, Skaði, Jörð ok Iðunn, Ilmr, Bil, Njörun."	*23. "Now shall the goddesses all be named: Frigg and Freyja, Fulla and Snotra, Gerdr and Gefjon, Gna, Lofn, Skadi, Jord and Idunn, Ilmr, Bil, Njorun."*

Scholars have theorised that since Snotra does not appear in any texts outside of the *Prose Edda*, she could in fact be an invention of Snorri Sturluson, or that Snorri had access to a lost source, and the little information about her could be inferred from her name.

Sol (Goddess of the Sun)

Sol (Sól, Sunna, Alfrodull) is the goddess or personification of the sun. She is the sister of Mani (the personification of the moon), and the daughter of Mundilfari (a god of light and the dawn).

According to the second of the two Merseburg Incantations known as 'the Horse Cure', written in 10th century Old High German, Sol also has a sister called Sinthgunt. Both Sol and Sinthgunt sing charms in order to heal a horse belonging to Phol, a figure equated with Baldr.

"Phol ende uuodan uuorun zi holza.	"Phol and Wodan were riding to the woods,
du uuart demo balderes uolon sin uuoz birenkit.	and the foot of Balder's foal was sprained
thu biguol en sinthgunt, sunna era suister;	So Sinthgunt, Sunna's sister, conjured it;
thu biguol en friia, uolla era suister;	and Frija, Volla's sister, conjured it;
thu biguol en uuodan, so he uuola conda:	and Wodan conjured it, as well he could:
sose benrenki, sose bluotrenki, sose lidirenki:	Like bone-sprain, so blood-sprain, so joint-sprain:
ben zi bena, bluot zi bluoda,	Bone to bone, blood to blood,
lid zi geliden, sose gelimida sin.	joints to joints, so may they be glued.

Sol is sometimes referred to by the poetic name or kenning Alfrodull (Álfröðull, 'elf-beam', 'elf-disc', 'elf-glory', or 'elf-heaven'), which refers to the sun herself and to the chariot that she rides across the sky. Her chariot is pulled by two horses Arvakr (Árvakr, 'early-awake') and Alsvidr (Alsviðr, 'very-quick'). The chariot is chased by the wolf Sköll, who during the events of Ragnarök ('the Twilight of the Gods') catches up with Sol and devours her.

Syn (Goddess of Defence and Refusal)

Syn is a goddess associated with defence and refusal. Her name comes from the Old Norse word '*synja*' ('to deny', 'to refuse'), from the Proto-Germanic '*sunjōną*'. In the *Prose Edda* in *Gylfaginning* ('The Beguiling of Gylfi'), Syn is listed among the gods and goddesses, and described as one who protects the door to the hall.

> *"Ellifta Syn, hon gætir dura í höllinni ok lýkr fyrir þeim, er eigi skulu inn ganga, ok hon er sett til varnar á þingum fyrir þau mál, er hon vill ósanna. Því er þat orðtak, at syn sé fyrir sett, þá er maðr neitar."*

> "The eleventh is Syn: she keeps the door in the hall, and locks it before those, who should not go in; she is also set at trials as a defence against such suits as she wishes to refute: then is the expression, that syn is set forward, when a man denies."

Syn is also mentioned in the *Prose Edda* in *Skáldskaparmál* ('The Language of Poetry'), in a subsection called *Nafnaþulur* ('Name-Rhapsody'). The poem lists the names of all of the figures in Norse Mythology by category (e.g: sea kings, giants, troll-wives, sons of Odin, members of the *Æsir*, etc.).

> *24. Hlín ok Nanna,*
> *Hnoss, Rindr ok Sjöfn,*
> *Sól ok Sága,*
> *Sigyn ok Vör.*
> *Þá er Vár, ok Syn*
> *verðr at nefna,*
> *en Þrúðr ok Rán*
> *þeim næst talið.*

> 24. Hlin and Nanna,
> Hnoss, Rindr and Sjofn,
> Sol and Saga,
> Sigyn and Vor.
> There is Var, and Syn
> needs to be named,
> and Thrudr and Ran
> are numbered next after them.

Var (Goddess of Oaths and Agreements)

Var (Vár, Vór) is a goddess associated with oaths and agreements.

Her name in Old Norse means either 'pledge' or 'beloved'.

In the *Poetic Edda* in Þrymskviða ('Thrim's Poem'), the blessing of Var is invoked by the *jötunn* (giant) Thrymr after his 'bride' (who is actually Thor disguised as Freyja) is hallowed with Thor's stolen hammer *Mjollnir*, at their wedding.

30. Þá kvað þat Þrymr, þursa dróttinn:
"Berið inn hamar brúði at vígja,
lekkið Mjöllni í meyjar kné,
vígið okkr saman Várar hendi."

30: Then loud spoke Thrym, the giants' leader:
"Bring in the hammer to hallow the bride;
On the maiden's knees let Mjollnir lie,
That us both the band of Vor may bless."

After this, Thor laughs internally, grabs *Mjollnir*, and kills Thrym and all his assembled family and following.

Var is mentioned in the *Prose Edda* in Gylfaginning ('The Beguiling of Gylfi') as one of the *Ásynjur* (the female goddesses of the *Æsir* family of gods). She is described as listening to people's oaths and private agreements.

"Níunda Vár, hon hlýðir á eiða manna ok einkamál, er veita sín á milli konur ok karlar. Því heita þau mál várar. Hon hefnir ok þeim, er brigða."

"The ninth is Var: she harkens to the oaths and compacts made between men and women; wherefore such covenants are called vows. She also takes vengeance on those who perjure themselves."

Var is also mentioned in the *Prose Edda* in Skáldskaparmál ('The Language of Poetry'), in a subsection called *Nafnaþulur* ('Name-Rhapsody'). The poem lists the names of all of the figures in Norse Mythology by category (e.g: sea kings, giants, troll-wives, sons of Odin, members of the *Æsir*, etc.).

24. "Hlín ok Nanna,
Hnoss, Rindr ok Sjöfn,
Sól ok Sága,
Sigyn ok Vör.
Þá er Vár, ok Syn
verðr at nefna,
en Þrúðr ok Rán
þeim næst talið."

24. "Hlin and Nanna,
Hnoss, Rindr and Sjofn,
Sol and Saga,
Sigyn and Vor.
There is Var, and Syn
needs to be named,
and Thrudr and Ran
are numbered next after them."

Vor (Goddess of Wisdom)

Vor (Vǫr, Vör) is a goddess associated with wisdom. Her name in Old Norse possibly means 'the careful one', 'aware', 'careful'. In the *Prose Edda* in *Gylfaginning* ('The Begyling of Gylfi'), Har gives descriptions of 16 *Ásynjur* (female goddesses of the *Æsir*), in which Vor is described as wise and of searching spirit, and that no one can conceal anything from her.

"Tíunda Vör, *hon er vitr ok spurul, svá at engi hlut má hana leyna.* *Þat er orðtak, at kona verði vör þess, er hon verðr vís."*	"The tenth is Vor: she is wise and of searching spirit, so that none can conceal anything from her; it is a saying, that a woman becomes 'aware' of that of which she is informed."

Vor is also mentioned in the *Prose Edda* in *Skáldskaparmál* ('The Language of Poetry'), in a subsection called *Nafnaþulur* ('Name-Rhapsody', in the section called *Ásynjur* (Goddesses):

Vor is also mentioned in the *Prose Edda* in *Skáldskaparmál* ('The Language of Poetry'), in a subsection called *Nafnaþulur* ('Name-Rhapsody'). The poem lists the names of all of the figures in Norse Mythology by category (e.g: sea kings, giants, troll-wives, sons of Odin, members of the *Æsir*, etc.).

24. "Hlín ok Nanna, Hnoss, Rindr ok Sjöfn, *Sól ok Sága, Sigyn ok Vör.* *Þá er Vár, ok Syn verðr at nefna, en Þrúðr ok Rán þeim næst talið."*	24. "Hlin and Nanna, Hnoss, Rindr and Sjofn, Sol and Saga, Sigyn and Vor. There is Var, and Syn needs to be named, and Thrudr and Ran are named next after them."

03 The Vanir

Freyja (Goddess of Love, Beauty, Fertility, War, Gold, and Magic)

Freyja (Freya, Freja) is a member of the *Vanir*. She is associated with seidr ('seiðr', a kind of magic for seeing and influencing the future).

Her name in Old Norse means 'lady' or 'the lady', from the Proto-Germanic '*frawjǭ*', and similar to the Old English '*frēo*', '*frōwe*', Old Frisian '*frowe*', Old Saxon '*frūa*', and Old High German '*frouwa*' (compare the modern German '*frau*', and the Dutch '*vrouw*').

Freyja is the daughter of Njord and the unnamed sister-wife of Njord, and the twin-sister of Freyr. She is also the wife of Odr (Óðr) and together they have two children, Hnoss ('jewel' or 'gem') and Gersemi ('treasure').

Odr is frequently absent from Freyja, often away on long journeys, and while he is away from her she cries tears of red gold for him and searches for him under different assumed names, such as Gefn ('the giver'), Horn ('flaxen-one'), Mardoll ('sea-brightener'), Syr ('sow'), Vanadís ('the Dis' or 'goddess of fate' of the *Vanir*), and Valfreyja ('Freyja of the slain').

Scholars debate whether Freyja and the goddess Frigg are both versions of an older single goddess worshipped across all of the Germanic peoples, and whether the goddess Gefjon is linked with her epithet or pseudonym Gefn.

In the Poetic Edda in *Grímnismál* ('The Lay of Grímnir'), Odin (disguised as Grímnir) tells the young Agnar of a number of mythological locations. Freyja rules over her heavenly meadow or field called *Fólkvangr* ('field of the host'), where she receives half of those who die in battle (the other half go to Odin's hall Valhalla). Within *Fólkvangr* is Freyja's hall called *Sessrúmnir* ('seat-room').

14. "Fólkvangr er inn níundi, en þar Freyja ræðr
sessa kostum í sal;
halfan val hon kýss hverjan dag,
en halfan Óðinn á."

14. "Fólkvangr is the ninth, where there Freyja decides
who shall merit seats in the hall;
half of the chosen she chooses every day,
and half Odin has."

She also assists other deities by allowing them to use her feathered cloak, and she is traditionally invoked and prayed to in matters of fertility and love. Frequently sought after as a wife by the *Jötnar* (giants), Freyja owns a necklace called *Brísingamen* ('fire' or 'amber necklace' or 'necklace of the Brisings'). When Freyja learns that the giant Thrymr (Þrymr, 'noise', 'crash') wants to marry her in return for Thor's hammer Mjolnir ('lightning') which he has previously stolen, the necklace shivers.

Freyja is mentioned in the Poetic Edda in *Völuspá* ('The Prophecy of the Völva'), *Grímnismál* ('The Lay of Grimnir'), *Lokasenna* ('Loki's Verbal Duel'), *Þrymskviða* ('Thrim's Poem'), *Oddrúnargrátr* ('Oddrún's Lament'), and *Hyndluljóð* ('The Lay of Hyndla').

Freyja is also mentioned in the Prose Edda in *Skáldskaparmál* ('The Language of Poetry'), and here in Gylfaginning ('The Beguiling of Gylfi'):

En Freyja er ágætust af ásynjum.	And Freyja is the most renowned of the Ásynjur.
Hon á þann bæ á himni, er Fólkvangr heitir.	she has there a dwelling in heaven Fólkvangr named,
Ok hvar sem hon ríðr til vígs, þá á hon hálfan val, en hálfan Óðinn, svá sem hér segir:	and where that she rides to battle, then has she half of the slain, and half Odin, so as here is said:
Folkvangr heitir, *en þar Freyja ræðr* *sessa kostum í sal;* *halfan val* *hon kýss hverjan dag,* *en halfan Óðinn á.*	Fólkvangr it is called, where there Freyja rules seats of merit in the hall; half the slain she keeps each day, and half Odin has.
Salr hennar Sessrúmnir, hann er mikill ok fagr.	The hall of hers is called Sessrúmnir, it is great and fair.
En er hon ferr, þá ekr hon köttum tveim ok sitr í reið.	When that she travels, then drives her two cats and sits in her chariot.
Hon er nákvæmust mönnum til á at heita, ok af hennar nafni er þat tignarnafn, er ríkiskonur eru kallaðar fróvur.	She is most agreeable to peoples prayers, and of her name comes the name of honour, by which noblewomen are called, Frú.
Henni líkaði vel mansöngr.	She likes well the songs of people.
Á hana er gott at heita til ásta."	Of her it is good to swear to love".

Freja by John Bauer, 1905
Creative Commons, Public Domain

Freyr (God of Kingship, Fertility, Prosperity, and Peace)

Freyr (Frey, Ingunar-Freyr, Yngvi-Freyr, Yngvi) is a member of the *Vanir*. His name in Old Norse means 'lord', which is comparable to the Gothic '*frauja*', the Old English '*frēa*', and Old High German '*frō*', all of which come from the Proto-Norse '**frawjaʀ*', and the Proto-Germanic '**frawjazoʀ*' or '**fraw(j)ōn*'. He is also known by his much older name Yngvi, from the Proto-Germanic '*Ingwaz*'.

Freyr is the son of Njord and the unnamed sister-wife of Njord. He is also the twin-brother of Freyja. According to the Poetic Edda in *Grímnismál* ('The Lay of Grimnir'), the gods give Freyr the place *Alfheim* ('Realm of the Elves', literally 'Elf-Home') as a teething gift:

"*Alfheim Frey gáfu í árdaga tívar at tannféi.*"

"Alfheim, Freyr was given, in ancient times, by the gods, as a teething-gift."

Freyr rides a boar named *Gullinbursti* ('gold mane' or 'golden bristles'), which has golden bristles in its mane that glow in the dark. *Gullinbursti* was made for Freyr as a gift by two dwarves named Sindri (or Etri) and Brokkr. This is described in the Prose Edda in *Skáldskaparmál* ('The Language of Poetry').

"*Þá lagði Sindri svínskinn í aflinn ok bað blása Brokk ok létta eigi fyrr en hann tæki þat ór aflinum, er hann hafði í lagt.*

En þegar er hann var genginn ór smiðjunni, en hinn blés, þá settist fluga ein á hönd honum ok kroppaði, en hann blés sem áðr, þar til er smiðrinn tók ór aflinum, ok var þat göltr, ok var burstin ór gulli.

Þá bar fram Brokkr sína gripi...
En Frey gaf hann göltinn ok sagði, at hann mátti renna loft ok lög nótt ok dag meira en hverr hestr ok aldri varð svá myrkt af nótt eða í myrkheimum, at eigi væri ærit ljós, þar er hann fór; svá lýsti af burstinni."

"Then laid Sindri the pigskin in the hearth and asked Brokk to blow and let up not before he had taken it out of the hearth, which he had there laid.
But then when he was going out of the smithy, but the other blew, then settled a fly on hand his and bit his body, but he blew as before there until the smith took it out of the hearth, and it was a boar, and were the bristles out of gold.
Then brought forward Brokkr his gifts...
To Freyr gave he the boar and said, that he may run through the air and light the night and day more than any horse, and never would be so murky of night or in the home of darkness, that not would he be frustrated of light, there where he travelled, so the delight of his bristles".

Freyr owns a ship called *Skíðblaðnir* ('assembled of wood'), the finest of ships, which always has a favourable breeze and can be folded up as if it were a cloth into one's pocket or a pouch when not needed.

The 11th century German medieval chronicler Adam of Bremen, in his Latin work *Gesta Hammaburgensis Ecclesiae Pontificum* ('Deeds of the Bishops of Hamburg'), describes pagan practices in Sweden. He refers to Freyr with the Latinised name Fricco and mentions an image of him at Skara (Västra Götaland County, Sweden):

"In hoc templo, quod totum ex auro paratum est, statuas atrium deorum veneratur populus, ita ut potentissimus eorum Thor in medio solium habeat triclinio; hinc et inde locum possident Wodan et Fricco."...

..."*Tertius est Fricco, pacem voluptatem que largiens mortalibus.*"

"In this temple, which in all out of gold is prepared, statues in the court of the gods were venerated by the people, so as the most powerful of them, Thor, in the middle of the floor of the chamber, on either side they sit Wodan and Fricco."...

..."The third is Fricco, peace and pleasure which bestows on mortals."

Snorri Sturluson mentions Freyr as one of the major gods in the Prose Edda in *Gylfaginning* ('The Beguiling of Gylfi'):

"Freyr er hinn ágætasti af ásum. Hann ræðr fyrir regni ok skini sólar, ok þar með ávexti jarðar, ok á hann er gott at heita til árs ok friðar. Hann ræðr ok fésælu manna."

"Freyr is the most renowned of the Æsir. He rules over the rain and shining sun, and there with the the growings of the earth, and it is of him good to call upon for the seasons and for peace. He rules also the prosperity of people."

Also in the Prose Edda is the story of Freyr falling in love with and eventually marrying the beautiful giantess Gerdr. In the process of courting Gerdr and obtaining the promise of her hand in marriage, Freyr gives up his sword (which fights on its own if the one using it is wise). Having bargained away his sword, Freyr is later forced to fight the jötunn Belli armed with an antler. Freyr successfully defeats Belli without his sword, but during the events of *Ragnarök* ('the Twilight of the Gods'), Freyr is killed by the fire *jötunn* Surtr ('the dark one', or 'the swarthy one').

The final battle between Freyr and Surtr by Lorenz Frølich, 1895
Creative Commons, Public Domain

Gullveig (The Golden Sorceress)

Gullveig (Heidr, Heiðr) is a member of the *Vanir*. The meaning the name Gullveig in Old Norse is uncertain.

The first part of her name is '*gull-*' ('gold') The second part '-*veig*' is uncertain (it also appears in the names Rannveig, Sölveig, and Thórveig).

Theories on the meaning of her name range from 'power', 'strength', 'intoxicating drink', 'lady', 'gold', 'gold thread', 'gold-drink', 'gold drunk', 'gold-draught'.

Gullveig is sometimes believed to be a personification of gold itself, purified through repeated smelting (death and rebirth). Her later name Heidr (Heiðr) means 'bright' or 'clear'.

She appears in the *Æsir-Vanir War*. In the Poetic Edda in *Völuspá* ('The Prophecy of the Völva') she comes to the hall of Odin where she is speared by the *Æsir*, burnt three times, and reborn three times.

On her third rebirth, she begins practising seidr (seiðr, a kind of magic for seeing and influencing the future) and takes the name Heidr (Heiðr).

Scholars have proposed that Gullveig / Heidr was once the same figure as the goddess Freyja, and that Gullveig's treatment at the hands of the *Æsir* may have been one of the events that led to the *Æsir-Vanir War*.

The fact that she is described as the "wide-seeing witch" and a "joy" to "evil women", suggests that she was well-known as a practitioner of different kinds of magic before she sought out the home of the *Æsir*, and that the *Æsir* mistrusted her and saw her as a threat, fearing that she would bewitch them somehow.

21." Þat man hon fólkvíg fyrst í heimi, er Gullveig geirum studdu	21. "The war I remember, the first in the world, When the gods with spears had smitten Gollveig,
ok í höll Hárs hana brendu; þrysvar brendu þrysvar borna, opt, ósjaldan, þó hon enn lifir.	And in the hall of Hor had burned her, Three times burned, and three times born, Oft and again, yet ever she lives.
22. Heiði hana hétu, hvars til húsa kom,	22. Heithi they named her who sought their home,
völu velspá, vitti hon ganda, seið hon hvars hon kunni, seið hon hugleikin, æ var hon angan illrar brúðar."	The wide-seeing witch, in magic wise; Minds she bewitched that were moved by her magic, To evil women a joy she was."

Kvasir (Poet, Scholar, and Wisest of All)

Kvasir is a god of poetry and wisdom. The name Kvasir is believed to be related to the name of a juice squeezed from berries and then fermented in some ancient cultures.

The origin, downfall, and legacy of Kvasir are described in *Skáldskaparmál* ('The Language of Poetry').

Ægir asks the skaldic god Bragi where the craft of poetry originated. Bragi says that the *Æsir* once had fought with the *Vanir* but eventually they came together to make peace.

The *Æsir* and *Vanir* decide to form a truce by way of both sides spitting into a vat. After they leave, the gods keep the vat as a symbol of their truce.

Out of the contents of the vat, they make a man who is named Kvasir. He is extremely wise and he knows the answer to any question posed to him.

Kvasir travels far and wide throughout the world teaching mankind and spreading his vast knowledge.

After a while, two dwarves who are brothers, named Fjalar and Galar, invite Kvasir to their home for a private talk. Upon Kvasir's arrival, the two dwarfs kill Kvasir and drain his blood into three objects.

Two of the objects are vats, called Son and Bodn, and the third is a pot called Odrerir (Óðrerir). Fjalar and Galar mix the blood with honey and make mead out of it. Whoever drinks the mead becomes a poet or scholar (Kvasir's blood is called *Skáldskaparmjöðr*, 'The Mead of Poetry').

The two dwarves explain to the *Æsir* that Kvasir has died from "suffocating in his own intelligence", as none of them are so well educated as to be able to pose him questions. Bragi then tells how the Mead of Poetry, by way of the god Odin, ultimately comes into the hands of mankind.

Also in *Skáldskaparmál*, among the various poetic terms or kennings is a term for poetry, which is given as "Kvasir's Blood'.

Kvasir is mentioned in Gylfaginning ('The Beguiling of Gylfi') in an account of how Loki is captured by the gods before being punished for the deatlh of Baldr.

Loki is hiding from the gods in his mountain lookout house, considering what sort of device the gods might use to capture him. He knots together several pieces of linen thread and invents what will from then on be known as a net.

When Loki senses that the gods are near, he throws the net on the fire and slips into a nearby river. Kvasir, "the wisest of all", is the first to enter Loki's house. He notices the outline of the net in the fire and realises its purpose. Kvasir tells the gods about what he has seen, and the gods use the shape as their model, making their own net and fishing Loki from the river.

Njord (God of the Sea)

Njord (Njǫrðr, Njörðr, Njörður, Njor, Njoerd, Njorth) is a member of the *Vanir*, but he later joined the *Æsir*. With his unnamed sister-wife, he is the father of Freyr and Freyja. He lives in Noatun (ship-enclosure) in the heavens. He is worshipped by seafarers wishing for good weather and calm seas, and by fishermen hoping for a bountiful catch of fish. He is also associated with crops and crop fertility.

The name Njord corresponds to the name of the older Germanic fertility goddess *Nerthus* from the Proto-Germanic '*Nerþuz'. It is possible that Njord and Nerthus (or *Njörun*) were a divine pairing, with similar names from a common root, and that the unnamed sister-wife of Njord could in fact be a version of Nerthus or Njörun that has been lost over time.

Some Old Icelandic translations of Classical mythology have Njord suggested as an equivalent to the god Saturn (rather than Neptune as one might expect). Njord has some similarities with Beika-Galles (The Old Man of the Winds), a god of rain and wind in Saami mythology, according to Gylfaginning ('The Beguiling of Gylfi') and the descriptions of Beika-Galles in the reports of missionaries in the 18th century. These similarities are believed to be due to contact between the Saami and seafaring Norsemen across Norway, Sweden, Finland, and the Kola Peninsula in Russia.

Njord is mentioned in the Poetic Edda in *Vafþrúðnismál ('the Lay of Vafþrúðnir')*. Odin (under the name Gagnráðr) is engaged in a contest of knowledge with the *jötunn* named Vafthrudnir. Odin asks Vafthrudnir from where Njord came to the *Æsir*.

Óðinn kvað:
38. "Seg þú þat it tíunda,
alls þú tíva rök
öll, Vafþrúðnir, vitir,
hvaðan Njörðr of kom
með ása sonum -
hofum ok hörgum
hann ræðr hundmörgum -
ok varð-at hann ásum alinn."

Vafþrúðnir kvað:
39. "Í Vanaheimi
skópu hann vís regin
ok seldu at gíslingu goðum,
í aldar rök
hann mun aftr koma
heim með vísum vönum."

Odin spoke:
38. "Say-you that tenth,
since you the gods history
all, Vafthrudnir, know,
where from did Njord come
with the sons of the *Æsir* -
temples and shrines
he ruled hundred-many -
and was that he of the *Æsir* born."

Vafthrudnir spoke:
39. "In Vanaheim
created in him wise ruling,
in old history
he will come back
home with the wise *Vanir*".

In *Grímnismál* ('The Lay of Grímnir'), Njord is described as having a hall in Noatun which he made himself. He is also described as a ruler of men who is without malice, who rules from a high timbered temple.

16. Nóatún eru in elliftu,	16. Noatun is the eleventh,
en þar Njörðr hefir,	where there Njord has;
sér of görva sali;	himself of made a hall;
manna þengill inn meins vani	of men a king, without malice
hátimbruðum hörgi ræðr.	highly-timbered temple ruling.

The poem also mentions the creation of Freyr's ship *Skíðblaðnir* by the Sons of Ivaldi, a group of dwarves who are masters of craft. Freyr is named as the son of Njord.

43. Ívalda synir gengu í árdaga	43. In days of old did Ivaldi's sons
Skíðblaðni at skapa,	Skithblathnir fashion fair,
skipa bezt, skírum Frey,	The best of ships for the bright god Freyr,
nýtum Njarðar bur.	The noble son of Njord.

In the Old Norse poem *Sólarljóð* written in Iceland around the year 1200, it is told that there are runes revealing the names of Njord's nine daughters, but only the names of the eldest and the youngest are given in the poem:

79. "Hér eru rúnar,	79. "Here there are runes,
sem ristit hafa	which written have
Njarðar dætr níu:	Njord's daughters nine:
Böðveig hin elzta	Bodveig the eldest
ok Kreppvör hin yngsta	and Kreppvor the youngest
ok þeira systr sjau."	and their sisters seen."

In the Prose Edda in Gylfaginning ('The Beguiling of Gylfi'), Njord is introduced as "third among the *Æsir*", dwelling in his home Noatun in the heavens. He rules the winds, calms seas and fires. Men call on him "for voyages and for hunting". He is "not of the race of *Æsir*", but raised in the home of the *Vanir*. He was delivered to the *Æsir* as a hostage in peace negotiations at the end of the *Æsir-Vanir* war. Njord's marriage to his first wife Skadi is also described, during which they attempt to divide their time between Skadi's home of Thrymheimr and Njord's home Noatun, however they soon discover that they are ill-suited to each other's homes. Njord finds the hills and the wailing of wolves loathsome, and Skadi cannot sleep on the sea beds for the wailing of waterfowl.

Njörd's desire of the Sea by W G Collingwood, 1908
Creative Commons, Public Domain

04 The Jotnar (Giants)

Aegir (Ægir)

Personification of the sea.
Associated with brewing ale.
Husband of the goddess Ran.
Father of the Nine Daughters of Ægir and Rán (waves) and Snaer (snow).
Also known as Hler.

Alvaldi (Ölvaldi)

The 'all-powerful' one.
Father of Thjazi, Gangr and Idi.
Described as "very rich in gold".
His sons divide his inheritance by taking mouthfuls of his gold.

Angrboda (Angrboða)

'One who brings grief', 'she who offers sorrow', 'harm-bidder', 'mother of monsters'.
Wife of Loki.
Mother of Fenrir, Jormungandr, and Hel.

Aurboda (Aurboða)

'Gravel-bidder', 'gravel offerer'.
Wife of Gymir.
Mother of Gerdr.

Baugi

'Ring-shaped'.
Brother of Suttungr.

Beli

'Bellower' or 'roarer'.
Brother of Gerdr.
Killed by Freyr with an antler.

Bergelmir

'Bear-yeller', 'mountain-yeller', 'bare-yeller', or 'he who roars like a bear'.
Son of Thrudgelmir.

Bestla

Mother of Odin, Vili, and Ve.
Daughter (or granddaughter) of Bolthorn.

Bolthorn

'Evil-thorn'.
Father (or grandfather) of Bestla.

Býleistr

'Storm', 'storm-relieving', 'storm-flasher', or 'violent storm'.
Brother of Loki.

Eggther

Herdsman of a female jötunn (probably Angrboda).
Sitting on a mound, playing his harp, while the red rooster Fjalarr cock-crows to herald the onset of Ragnarök.

Farbauti

'Dangerous striker', 'anger striker', or 'sudden striker'.
Father of Loki.

Fjolvar

'Very wary', 'very cautious'.
Spends time fighting and seducing women with on the island of Algrœn ('All-Green').

Fornjot

'Ancient giant', 'primordial giant', 'original owner', 'destroyer', 'one who enjoys sacrifices', or 'ancient screamer'.
Father of Hlér ('sea'), Logi ('fire') and Kári ('wind').

Gangr

'Traveller'.
Son of Alvaldi.
Brother of Thjazi and Idi.
Gangr and his brothers received their father Alvaldi's rich inheritance by taking a mouthful of gold.

Geirrodr (Geirröðr)

'Spear-reddener'. Father of Gjalp and Greip.

Gillingr

'The screamer'. Father of Sutungr. Murdered by Fjalar and Galar.

Gjalp and Greip (Gjálp and Greip)

'Screamer' and 'Grasper'. Daughters of Geirrod. They are killed by Thor for trying to kill him.

Gridr

'Vehemence', 'Violence', 'Impetuous'. Mother of Vidarr. Gave Thor her belt of strength, iron glove, and staff Gridarvol.

Gunnlod

Daughter of Suttungr. Turned into a witch by her father. Guards the Mead of Poetry in the mountain called Hnitbjorg.

Gymir

'The earthly','the wintry one', 'the protector', or 'the engulfer'. Husband of Aurboda. Father of Gerdr.

Hardgreipr

'Hard-grip'. Daughter of Vagnophtus (according to Saxo Grammaticus in his Gesta Danorum).

Helblindi

'Helblind'. Brother of Loki and Byleistr.

Helreginn

'Hel-ruler', 'Hel-power', and 'Ruler of Hel'.
Named in Nafnaþulur (Skáldskaparmál, Prose Edda).
No additional information remains.

Hljod

Wife of Volsung, the ancestor of the Volsung family. Daughter of Hrimnir. Mother of Sigmund and Signy, heroes in the Volsung Saga.

Hraesvelgr (Hræsvelgr)

'Corpse-swallower', 'shipwreck-current'. Portrayed as an eagle shaped originator of the wind.

Hrimgerdr

'Frost-Gerda'. Daughter of Hati.

Hrimgrimnir

'Frost-masked'.
In Skírnismál ('The Lay of Skírnir'), Skirnir threatens Gerdr with a curse involving her marriage to Hrímgrímnir in Hel.

Hrimnir

'Frosty', 'the one covered with frost'. Father of Hljod.

Hrodr (Hroðr)

'Famed', 'the famed one', 'glorious', 'the glorious one'. Adversary of Thor.

Hrungnir

'Brawler'.
Made of stone.
Owns a horse named Gullfaxi.
Loses a horse race with Odin on Sleipnir.
Killed by Thor.

Hrymr

Plays a key role in the events of Ragnarök. Leads legions of giants towards the field of Vigridr to battle with the gods.

Hymir

Father of Tyr (according to Hymiskviða).
Owner of a brewing-cauldron fetched by Thor for Aegir who wants to hold a feast for the Æsir.
Goes fishing with Thor, they nearly catch the World Serpent Jormungandr.

Hyrrokkin

'Fire-withered', 'fire-steamer'.
Launched Baldr's ship Hringhorni at his funeral after the Æsir were unable to launch it.

Idi

'Active one', 'hard-working one'.
Son of Alvaldi.
Brother of Gangr and Thjazi.
With his brothers they received their father's rich inheritance by taking a mouthful of gold.

Imr (Ím)

'Dust'.
Son of Vafthrudnir.

Jarnsaxa

'Iron-dagger', 'armed-with-an-iron-sword'.
Thor's lover.
Mother of Magni.

Laufey

'Leaves', 'Foliage', possibly from Proto-Norse tree goddess called *lauf-awiaz ('leafy', 'the leafy', or 'the leafy one').
Mother of Loki.

Leikn

'Trickery', 'bewitchment', 'sorceress'.
Killed by Thor.

Litr (Lit)

'Colour', 'hue', or 'apearance'.
Mentioned as a poetic name or kenning for Thor: "Lit's men's fight-challenger".

Logi

The personification of fire.
Son of Fornjotr.
Brother of Aegir and Kari.
Marries fire giantess Glod.
Father of Eisa and Eimyrja.

Mogthrasir (Mögþrasir)

'The one who is striving for sons'.

Narfi (Nǫrfi, Nörfi)

The father of Nott (personification of night).

Sokkmimir (Sökkmímir)

Mentioned in Ynglingatal: underground homes of the jötnar are called "Sokkmimir's halls". Killed by Odin.

Surtr

The greatest of the fire giants.
Guardian of Muspelheim ('The Realm of Fire').
In the events of Ragnarök he kills Freyr.
His flames engulf the world.

Suttungr

Son of Gillingr.
Tortures Fjalar and Galar and obtains the Mead of Poetry.
Turns his daughter into a witch to guard the mead in the centre of the mountain Hnitbjorg.

Thjazi

Son of Alvaldi.
Brother of Idi and Gangr.
With his brothers they received their father's rich inheritance by taking a mouthful of gold.
Kidnaps Idunn, and is killed by the Æsir.
Odin casts Thjazi's eyes into the heavens and turns them into stars.

Thokk (Þökk)

Presumed to be Loki in disguise.
Refuses to weep for the slain Baldr, forcing Baldr to remain in Hel.

Thrivaldi (Þrívaldi)

'Thrice-mighty'.
Killed by Thor.

Thrudgelmir (Þrúðgelmir)

'Strength Yeller'.
Son of Aurgelmir (Ymir).
Father of Bergelmir.

Thrymr (Þrymr)

Steals Thor's hammer Mjolnir.
Ransoms Mjolnir for Freyja's hand in marriage.
Killed by Thor disguised as freyja.

Utgarda-Loki (Útgarða-Loki)

'Loki of the Outyards'.
Ruler of the castle Útgarðr.
Also known as Skrymir.

Vafthrudnir (Vafþrúðnir)

'Mighty weaver', 'mighty in riddles'.
Very wise.
Loses a battle of knowledge with Odin.

Vidblindi (Víðblindi)

'Very blind'.
A giant who drew whales out of the sea like fishes.

Vornir (Vörnir)

Named in Nafnaþulur in the Prose Edda.

Vosud

'Wet and sleety'.
Father of Vindsvalr.
Grandfather of Vetr ('winter').
Personification of icy wind.

Ymir

Also known as Aurgelmir, Brimir, or Blainn.
A primeval being and ancestor of all jötnar.
Killed by Odin, Vili, and Ve.
The world is made of parts of his body.

05 The Dvergar (Dwarves)

Alviss (Alvíss)

'All-wise'. Is promised to Thor's daughter Thrudr in marriage, but Thor disapproves. Thor tests his wisdom, but keeps him talking until sunrise, which turns Alviss to stone.

Andvari

'Careful one', 'cautious spirit', 'gentle breeze'. Lives underneath a waterfall and can change himself into a pike. Has a magical ring called Andvaranaut. Loki catches him and steals his gold. Andvari then curses the gold to anyone who touches it.

Austri

'East', 'the one in the east'. One of the four dwarves who holds up the dome of the sky after it is made out of Ymir's skull.

Billingr

'Twin brother'. The father of an unnamed maiden desired by Odin. Billingr thwarts Odin's attempts to see her by blocking Odin's path to her with warriors, swords, and burning torches.

Brokkr

'Blacksmith', 'the one who works with metal fragments'. Brother of Eitri or Sindri, the Sons of Ivaldi. Makes Thor's hammer Mjolnir with Eitri.

Dainn (Dáinn)

'The dead one', 'deadlike'. Described as a dwarf in some sources, and a king of elves in others. Introduces runes to the elves. Creates Freyja's boar Hlidisvini with Nabbi.

Durinn,

'Slumber', 'door', or 'door-warden'. Forges the magic sword Tyrfing with Dvalinn. The second dwarf after Motsognir.

Durnir (Dúrnir)

'Door', 'door-warden', 'sleeper'.

Dvalinn

'The dormant one', 'the one slumbering', 'torpid'. Introduces runes to the dwarves. Forges the magic sword Tyrfing with Durinn.

Eitri (Eitri)

'The very cold one'. Brother of Brokkr. One of the Sons of Ivaldi. Makes the golden boar Gullinbursti, the ring Draupnir, and the hammer Mjolnir.

Fafnir (Fáfnir)

'The embracer'. Kills his father Hreidmarr and takes his treasure. Dwells in the wilderness, taking the form of a dragon. Killed by Sigurd.

Fjalar and Galar

'Paneller' and 'Yeller', 'singer'. Kill Kvasir and turn his blood into the Mead of Poetry.

Gandalf

'Wand-elf', 'magic elf', 'wolf-elf'. A protective spirit wielding a magical wand.

Hreidmar (Hreiðmarr)

Sorcerer. Father of Regin, Fafnir, Otr, Lyngheidr, and Lofnheidr. Owned a house of glittering gold and flashing gems.

Ivaldi (Ívaldi)

'Wielder of the yew bow', 'warrior'. Father of the Sons of Ivaldi who make Freyr's ship Skidbladnir, Odin's spear Gungnir, and Sif's golden hair.

Litr

'Countenance', 'Image', 'complexion', 'colour'. Ran in front of Thor's feet during Baldr's funeral. Thor kicks him into the funeral pyre.

Motsognir (Mótsognir)

'He who roars in rage', 'he who drinks in might', 'he who drinks in courage'. Lord and ruler of all the Dwarves.

Nabbi

'Small boil'. Creates Freyja's boar Hlidisvini with Dainn.

Nordri

'North'. One of the four dwarves who holds up the dome of the sky after it is made out of Ymir's skull.

Otr (Ótr)

'Otter'. Son of Hreidmar and brother of Fafnir and Regin. Able to change into any form. Spends his days in the form of an otter eating fish.

Regin

'Great', 'vast', 'the potent one', 'the wielder'. Son of Hreidmar. Brother of Fafnir and Otr. Foster father of Sigurd.

Sons of Ivaldi

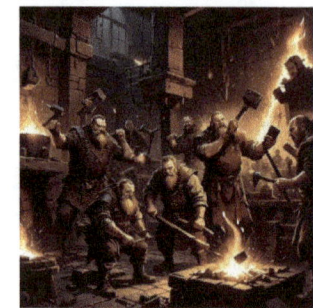

Sons of Ivaldi who make Freyr's ship Skidbladnir, Odin's spear Gungnir, and Sif's golden hair.

Sudri

'South'. One of the four dwarves who holds up the dome of the sky after it is made out of Ymir's skull.

Vestri

'West'. One of the four dwarves who holds up the dome of the sky after it is made out of Ymir's skull.

06 Others

Fenrir: The Giant Wolf

Fenrir (also Fenrisúlfr, Hróðvitnir, and Vánagandr) is a monstrous wolf. He is the offspring of Loki and female jötunn Angrboda.

His name in Old Norse means 'fen-dweller', and he is also referred to as Fenrisulfr 'Fenris-wolf', Hrodvitnir 'Fame-wolf', and Vanagandr 'Monster of the river Van'.

Fenrir plays a key role in the events of Ragnarök ('the Twilight of the Gods'). In the Prose Edda in Gylfaginning ('The Beguiling of Gylfi'), the gods are troubled by their knowledge of prophecies foretelling great trouble from the wolf Fenrir and his alarmingly rapid growth. It is foretold that Fenrir will kill Odin and assist in setting the world on fire.

The gods try to bind Fenrir with chains, under the ruse of encouraging him to test and demonstrate his strength for glory. The first chain is called Leyding, and the second is called Dromi, and Fenrir succeeds in breaking them both.

Fearing that they will never be able to bind Fenrir, Freyr's messenger Skírnir is sent to Niðavellir ('Down-vales'), also known as Myrkheimr ('Home of Darkness'), the home of the dwarvers, to commission the dwarves to forge a rope that is impossible to break.

The magic materials used in the making of this rope are: the sound of a cat's footfall, the beard of women, the roots of mountains, the sinews of the bear, the breath of the fish, and the spittle of the birds. The new rope is called Gleipnir ('the entangled one' or 'the deceiver') and is as thin as a silken ribbon but stronger than any iron chain.

As in their previous two attempts, the Æsir lure Fenrir to test his strength on this new rope. Fenrir insists on a pledge that they will not bind him permanently. Tyr places his right hand in Fenrir's mouth and the Æsir promise that they will let him go. Then when Fenrir realises that the Æsir will not release him, he bites off Tyr's hand at a location "now called the wolf's joint" (the wrist), causing Tyr to lose his right hand.

In the Poetic Edda in Völuspá ('The Prophecy of the Völva'), a völva tells Odin that his son Vidarr will avenge Odin's death at Ragnarök by stabbing Fenrir in the heart:

"Þá kemr inn mikli"
mögr Sigföður,
Víðarr, vega
at valdýri.
Lætr hann megi Hveðrungs

"Then comes the great
son victory-father,
Vidarr, to fight
against the beast.
he abates the son of Hveðrung (Loki)

mundum standa	he-will lay-upon
hjör til hjarta,	the sword to the heart
þá er hefnt föður."	then is avenged the father."

Later in Gylfaginning ('The Beguiling of Gylfi'), Vidarr's battle with Fenrir or the Fenris-wolf is described in more detail.

"Úlfrinn gleypir Óðin. Verðr þat hans bani.	"The Wolf shall swallow Odin; that shall be his ending
En þegar eftir snýst fram Víðarr ok stígr öðrum fæti í neðra kjöft úlfsins.	But straight thereafter shall Vídarr stride forth and set one foot upon the lower jaw of the Wolf:
Á þeim fæti hefir hann þann skó, er allan aldr hefir verit til samnat.	on that foot he has the shoe, materials for which have been gathering throughout all time.
Þat eru bjórar þeir, er menn sníða ór skóm sínum fyrir tám eða hæli.	(They are the scraps of leather which men cut out: of their shoes at toe or heel;
Því skal þeim bjórum braut kasta sá maðr, er at því vill hyggja at koma ásunum at liði.	therefore he who desires in his heart to come to the Æsir's help should cast those scraps away.)
Annarri hendi tekr hann inn efra kjöft úlfsins ok rífr sundr gin hans, ok verðr þat úlfsins bani.	With one hand he shall seize the Wolf's upper jaw and tear his gullet asunder; and that is the death of the Wolf.
Loki á orrostu við Heimdall, ok verðr hvárr annars bani.	Loki shall have battle with Heimdallr, and each be the slayer of the other.
Því næst slyngr Surtr eldi yfir jörðina ok brennir allan heim."	Then straightway shall Surtr cast fire over the earth and burn all the world"

Fenrir also has two offspring called Sköll ('one who mocks') and Hati ('one who hates'). Sköll chases the sun (the goddess Sól riding her chariot across the sky), and Hati chases the moon (the god Máni riding his chariot across the sky). During the events of Ragnarök ('the Twilight of the Gods'), they each catch their prey, and the sky and the earth darken and collapse.

Odin and Fenris by Mabel Dorothy Hardy, 1909
Creative Commons, Public Domain

Hel: Keeper of the Underworld

Hel is the keeper of the realm of the underworld with which she shares her name.

She receives a portion of the souls who have not been taken to Valhalla or Folkvangr.

The realm of Hel is located near Niflheim ('World of Mist', or 'Mist-Home').

Her name comes from the Proto-Germanic *haljō- meaning 'concealed place', or 'the underworld'.

Hel is the daughter of Loki and the female jötunn Angrboda (Angrboda's name translates as 'the one who brings grief' or 'she who offers sorrow' or 'harm bidder', and she is also referred to as a 'mother of monsters'). Hel is also the sister of Fenrir and Jormungandr.

When the gods find out that these three children of Loki and Angrboda are being brought up in Jötunheimr ('Realm of the Giants' literally 'Giant-Home'), they obtain prophecies that from these three siblings a great mischief and disaster will arise.

Odin sends the gods to gather these three children and bring them to him. When they arrive, Odin casts Hel into Niflheim ('Realm of Mists' or 'Mist Home') and gives her authority over nine worlds, in that she must 'administer board and lodging to those sent to her'.

In this realm Hel has "great mansions" with extremely high walls and immense gates, a hall called Éljúðnir ('sprayed with snowstorms' or 'damp with sleet or rain'), a dish called 'Hunger,' a knife called 'Famine,' the servant Ganglati ('lazy walker'), the serving-maid Ganglöt ('lazy walker'), the entrance threshold 'Stumbling-block', the bed 'Sick-bed,' and the curtains 'Gleaming-bale'.

Hel is described as "half black and half flesh-coloured" adding that this makes her easily recognizable, and furthermore that Hel is "rather downcast and fierce-looking".

In the Poetic Edda in Völuspá, Hel's realm is referred to as the "Halls of Hel". Also in the Poetic Edda in Grímnismál, Hel is listed as living beneath one of three roots growing from the world tree Yggdrasil.

In Baldrs Draumar ('Baldr's Dreams'), also known as Vegtamskviða ('The Lay of Vegtam'), Odin disguises himself as a wanderer named Vegtam and rides to the domain of Hel. He does not speak to Hel directly, instead he uses magic to awaken a völva (seeress) from her grave to ask her who will kill his son Baldr and who will avenge his death.

In the Prose Edda in Gylfaginning ('The Beguiling of Gylfi'), Hermodr rides to the realm of Hel and speaks to Hel herself, begging for Baldr's release from the underworld. Hel says that Baldr will only be released if all things, dead and alive, weep for him. All do except for a giantess named Þökk (Thokk, believed to be Loki in disguise), and so Baldr has to remain in the underworld.

Later on in Gylfaginning ('The Beguiling of Gylfi'), Har (Hár, 'High') describes the events of Ragnarök ('the Twilight of the Gods') and mentions a large field that is a hundred leagues in every direction called Vigridr (Vígríðr, 'battle-surge') or Oskopnir (Óskópnir, 'the not yet created').

It is foretold that the field Vigridr will host a great battle between the forces of the gods, and the forces of the jötunn Surtr ('black' or 'the swarthy one', the greatest of fire giants), and when Loki arrives at the battlefield, "all of Hel's people" will arrive with him.

Garm (Old Norse: Garmr) is the bloodstained hellhound who guards the gates of Hel (the underworld) at a cave called Gnipahellir ('Mountain Cave'). He is described as the most evil creature, and he is to wolves and dogs what Odin is to gods and what Yggdrasil is to trees, i.e. the greatest among them.

Hermod before Hela by John Charles Dollman 1909
Creative Commons, Public Domain

Jormungandr: The World Serpent

Jormungandr (Old Norse: Jǫrmungandr, Old Icelandic: Jörmungandur) also known as Miðgarðsormr ('The Midgard Serpent') is an immeasurably large sea serpent who lives in the world sea, encircling Midgard (the Earth) while biting his own tail.

His name in Old Norse can be translated as jǫrmun- = 'huge', 'vast' or 'superhuman' + gandr = 'elongated entity' or 'supernatural being', meaning 'the vast serpent' or 'the vast river' (a synonym for the world sea in which it lives).

Jormungandr is the middle child of Loki and the female jötunn Angrboda.

Thor has an ongoing feud with Jormungandr and during Ragnarök they fight each other to the death.

In one story, Thor encounters the giant king Útgarða-Loki and has to perform deeds for him, one of which is a challenge of Thor's strength.

Útgarða-Loki encourages Thor to attempting to lift the World Serpent, disguised by magic as a huge cat. Thor grabs the 'cat' (Jormungandr) around its midsection but manages to raise the cat only high enough for one of its paws to leave the floor.

Útgarða-Loki later explains his deception and that Thor's lifting the cat was an impressive deed, as he had stretched the serpent so that it had almost reached the sky.

Many watching became fearful when they saw one paw lift off the ground. If Thor had managed to lift the cat completely from the ground, he would have altered the boundaries of the universe.

Jormungandr and Thor meet again when Thor goes fishing with the giant Hymir. When Hymir refuses to provide Thor with bait, Thor strikes the head off Hymir's largest ox to use it.

Thor and Hymir row to a point where Hymir often sat and caught flatfish and where he drew up two whales. Thor demands to go further out to sea and does so despite Hymir's protest.

Thor then prepares a strong line and a large hook and baits it with the ox head, which Jormungandr bites. Thor pulls the serpent from the water, and the two face one another, Jormungandr blowing poisonous venom.

Hymir goes pale with fear. As Thor grabs his hammer to kill the serpent, Hymir cuts the line, leaving the serpent to sink beneath the waves and return to its original position encircling the earth.

23. Dró djarfliga dáðrakkr Þórr
orm eitrfáan upp at borði;
hamri knídi háfjall skarar
ofljótt ofan ulfs hnitbróður.

23. Drew boldly valiantly Thor
the serpent poisonous to the boards;
hammer struck high-mountain cuts
monstrous over the wolf's own brother.

*24. Hraungalkn hlumðu, en hölkn þutu,
fór in forna fold öll saman;
sökkðisk síðan sá fiskr í mar.*

24. Lava rocks roared, and sleet blew,
went into the ancient fold all together;
then sunk the fish into the sea.

In the Prose Edda in Gylfaginning, and in the Poetic Edda in Völuspá, one sign of the coming of Ragnarok is the violent unrest of the sea as Jormungandr releases its tail from its mouth.

The sea will flood and Jormungandr will thrash onto the land. It will advance, spraying poisonous venom to fill the air and water, beside Fenrir, whose eyes and nostrils blaze with fire and whose gape touches the earth and the sky.

They will join the sons of Muspell to battle the gods on the plain of Vigridr, where Thor will eventually kill Jormungandr but will then fall dead after walking nine paces, having been poisoned by the serpent's deadly venom.

*56
Þá kemr inn mæri
mögr Hlóðynjar,
gengr Óðins sonr
við orm vega,
drepr af móði
Miðgarðs véurr,
munu halir allir
heimstöð ryðja;
gengr fet níu
Fjörgynjar burr
neppr frá naðri
níðs ókvíðnum.*

56
Then comes the noble
son of Hlóðyn (the earth),
goes Odin's son
against the serpent to slay,
kills of rage
Midgard's Veor (Thor),
should all flee
homestead free;
walking steps nine
Mother earth's son (Thor)
overcome from the serpent
down fearless.

Thor and the Midgard Serpent by Emil Doepler, 1905
Creative Commons, Public Domain

The Nornir: The Three Fates

The Nornir are a trio of powerful maiden giantesses (jötnar) who are responsible for shaping the destinies of all gods and humans alike. They draw water and clay from the sacred well called Urðarbrunnr ('wellspring of Urdr') that lies beneath Yggdrasil ('the world tree') in order to nourish and protect Yggdrasil.

They are also believed to visit each newborn child in to determine their future. They can be either benevolent ('good-willing', kind, or protective) or malevolent ('bad-willing', causing tragic events).

The origin of the name norn is uncertain and may derive from a word meaning 'to twine', which would refer to their twining the threads of fate. Another theory suggests that the word norn is related to the Swedish dialect word norna (nyrna), a verb that means 'to communicate secretly', which suggests mysterious figures who only reveal the fate of a person as their fate comes to pass.

There are three Norns:
- Urdr (Urðr, Urd, Urth, 'fate', 'destiny', 'that which became or happened') from the Proto-Germanic *wurdiz
- Verdandi (Verðandi, Verdandi, Verthandi, 'happening', 'present', 'that which is becoming or happening') from verða ('to become', 'to happen'), from the Proto-Germanic *werþaną
- Skuld ('debt', 'obligation', 'that which should be or needs to happen'), from the Proto-Germanic *skuldiz

The Norns are mentioned in the Poetic Edda in Völuspá ('The Prophecy of the Völva'):

"Þaðan koma meyjar
margs vitandi

"Then come the maidens,
much in wisdom

þrjár, ór þeim sal	three, from their hall
er und þolli stendr;	which under patiently standing
Urð hétu eina,	Urd is named one,
aðra Verðandi,	another Verdandi,
skáru á skíði,	scoring on wood,
Skuld ina þriðju;	Skuld the third;
þær lög lögðu,	there law laid,
þær líf kuru	they life allotted
alda börnum,	to the sons of men
örlög seggja."	and said their fate."

In the Poetic Edda in Helgakviða Hundingsbana I ('The First Lay of Helgi Hundingsbane') the Norns visit the newly born hero Helgi Hundingsbane and decide his future:

Nótt varð í bæ,	Night was in the dwelling,
nornir kómu,	the Nornir came.
þær er öðlingi	They who posess
aldr of skópu;	ages of shaping;
þann báðu fylki	then bid battle
frægstan verða	famed become
ok buðlunga	and king
beztan þykkja.	the best thought of.

The Norns by Johannes Gehrts, 1889
Creative Commons, Public Domain

Yggdrasil: The World Tree

Yggdrasil is the giant sacred ash tree at the centre of the nine worlds: Midgard, the world of humanity, Asgard, the world of the Æsir gods and goddesses, Vanaheim, the world of the Vanir gods and goddesses, Jotunheim, the world of the giants, Niflheim, the primordial world of ice, Muspelheim, the primordial world of fire, Alfheim, the world of the elves, Nidavellir or Svartalfheim, the world of the dwarves, and Hel, the domain of the goddess Hel, the underworld.

The name Yggdrasil is generally accepted to mean 'Odin's Horse' where 'horse' is a euphemism for 'gallows', in reference to when Odin sacrificed himself by hanging from Yggdrasil for nine days. Yggr is one of Odin's many other names, and 'drasill' is a poetic term for horse, possibly from Proto-Indo-European *d^{h}er- ('to hold, support').

The branches of Yggdrasil extend far into the heavens, including Asgard, the home of the gods. The place where the branches extend into Asgard is the meeting place where the gods regularly hold their traditional governing assemblies.

Yggdrasil is supported by three roots that extend to three wells. The first of these roots extends to Urðarbrunnr ('Wellspring of Urd'), where the Nornir ('The Fates') set down laws and the fates and destinies of gods and humans. The Nornir draw water and clay from the spring, and then pour it over Yggdrasil to nourish and protect it. The water is described as so holy that anything that enters will become "as white as the membrane called the skin that lies round the inside of the eggshell". Two swans feed from the wellspring, from which all other swans descend.

Another root extends to Hvergelmir ('Bubbling Boiling Spring'), where liquid from the antlers of the stag Eikþyrnir flow into all of the rivers around where the Æsir live and beyond. Living in the spring are a vast amount of snakes and the dragon Níðhöggr ('Malice Striker') who gnaws at the root of Yggdrasil.

The third root extends to Mímisbrunnr ('Mimir's Wellspring') in Jötunheimr ('The Ream of the Giants', literally 'Giant-Home') where the primordial plane of Ginnungagap ('gaping abyss', 'yawning void') once existed at the beginning of creation. Mimir drinks from his well and gains great knowledge. Even after he is beheaded in the Æsir-Vanir war, his head continues to give Odin advice and wise counsel.

Yggdrasil is mentioned in the Poetic Edda in Völuspá ('The Prophecy of the Völva'):

19. Ask veit ek standa,	19. An as I know stands,
heitir Yggdrasill,	named Yggdrasil,
hár baðmr, ausinn	high tree, sprinkled
hvíta auri;	with white clay;
þaðan koma döggvar,	then come the dews,
þærs í dala falla,	there in the dale that fall,
stendr æ yfir grænn	standing forever over green
Urðarbrunni.	Urdr's wellspring.

Many creatures are said to live within Yggdrasil, including: Níðhöggr the dragon, an unnamed eagle, Ratatoskr ('drill tooth' or 'bore-tooth') a squirrel who runs up and down the branches to carry messages between Níðhöggr and the eagles perched on top, and the four stags Dáinn, Dvalinn, Duneyrr and Duraþrór who gnaw at the branches, and the morning dew gathers in their horns and forms the rivers of the world (like the stag Eikþyrnir in Hvergelmir).

Another creature who feeds on the branches of Yggdrasil is Heidrun (Heiðrún), a nanny goat who produces large quantities of mead from her udders which is then collected in cauldrons and served to the einherjar (those who have died in battle who are feasting at Valhalla).

Other names for Yggdrasil include Hoddmímis holt ('Hoard-Mimir's Tree'), Mímameidr (Mímameiðr, 'Mimir's Tree'), and Laerad (Læraðr, 'harm', 'betrayal', 'arranger of betrayal', or 'shelter', 'giver of protection').

The Ash Yggdrasil by Friedrich Wilhelm Heine, 1886
Creative Commons, Public Domain

07 Interesting Objects

Alfrodull	The chariot of the goddess Sol, pulled by two horses, Arvakr and Alsvidr across the sky each day. Translates as 'Elf-beam', 'Elf-disc', 'Elf-glory', 'Elf-heaven'
Andvaranaut	A magical ring capable of producing gold, first owned by Andvari.
Angrvadall	A magical sword inscribed with Runic letters which blaze in time of war but gleam with a dim light in time of peace. Translates as 'Stream of Anguish'.
Aurvandils-ta	Aurvandill's Toe. Thor throws Aurvandill's frozen toe into the sky to form a star.
Bifrost	A burning rainbow bridge that reaches between Midgard (the world) and Asgard (the realm of the gods).
Bodn	One of the vessels that contains the Mead of Poetry.
Bragi's Harp	A magical golden harp given to Bragi by the dwarves when he was born.
Brisingamen	The necklace of the goddess Freyja.
Dainsleif	A sword that gave wounds that never healed and could not be unsheathed without killing a man. Translatea as 'Dainn's legacy'.
Draupnir	A golden arm ring possessed by Odin that is a source of endless wealth.
Dromi	One of the chains forged by Thor to bind Fenrir, which broke.
Eitr	A liquid substance that is the origin of all living things, produced by Jormungandr and other serpents.
Fafnir's Blood	Sigurd drank some of Fafnir's blood and gained the ability to understand the language of the birds. Sigurd also bathed in dragon's blood that gave him invulnerability.
Fafnir's Heart	Roasted and consumed by Sigurd, which gave him the gift of prophecy.
Falcon Cloak	A cloak owned by Freyja that allows the wielder to turn into a falcon.
Forseti's Axe	A golden battle axe that Forseti used to save the old sages of the wreck, which he then threw to an island to bring forth a source of water. Also called Fosite's axe from Frisian mythology.
Freyja's Chariot	A chariot pulled by cats.
Freyr's Sword	A magic sword that would fight on its own if the wielder was wise enough.
Friggerock	Another name for Orion's Belt in astrology which rotates on the celestial equator. Translates as 'Frigg's distaff'.
Gjallarbru	A covered bridge which spans the river Gjoll and must be crossed in order to reach Hel. Translates as 'Gjoll Bridge'.

Gjallarhorn	A mystical horn blown at the onset of Ragnarok associated with the god Heimdallr and the wise being Mimir.
Gjoll	The rock to which Fenrir the wolf is bound.
Glasir	A tree or grove described as "the most beautiful among gods and men", bearing golden leaves located in the realm of Asgard, outside the doors of Valhalla. Translates as 'Gleaming'.
Gleipnir	The fetter that successfully binds the wolf Fenrir. It is light and thin as silk, but strong as creation itself and made from six impossible ingredients: the sound of a cat's footfall, the beard of women, the roots of mountains, the sinews of the bear, the breath of the fish, and the spittle of the birds.
Golden Coat of Chainmail	Part of Fafnir's treasure which Sigurd took after he slew the dragon.
Gram	The sword that Odin struck into the world tree Barnstokkr which only Sigmund the Volsung was able to pull out. It broke in battle with Odin but was later reforged by Sigmund's son Sigurd who used it to slay the dragon Fafnir. After being reforged, it could cleave an anvil in half.
Gridavolr	A magical staff given to Thor by Gridr so he could kill the giant Geirrod.
Grove of Nerthus	On an "island in the ocean" (Zealand, Denmark), Tacitus describes a sacred grove dedicated to the goddess Nerthus.
Grove of the Semnones	In Northern Germany, according to Tacitus, the Semnones allowed no one to enter the grove without being fettered and blindfolded.
Gungnir	Odin's spear, created by the Sons of Ivaldi. The spear is described as being so well balanced that it could strike any target, no matter the skill or strength of the wielder.
Helskor	Shoes that were put on the dead so that they could go to Valhalla. Translates as 'Hel-shoes'.
Hlidskjalf	Odin's all-seeing throne in his palace Valaskjalf. Known as 'the high seat with the wide view'.
Hofud	The sword of Heimdallr, the guardian of Bifrost.
Hringhorni	The ship of the god Baldr, described as the "greatest of all ships".
Hulidshjalmr	A concealing helmet of the dwarves.
Hvergelmir	Hvergelmir ('Bubbling Boiling Spring'), where liquid from the antlers of the stag Eikþyrnir flow into all of the rivers around where the Æsir live and beyond.
Hymir's Cauldron	A mile-wide cauldron which the Æsir wanted to brew beer in.
Jarngreipr	A pair of iron gauntlets used by Thor. Translates as 'Iron Grippers'.
Laedingr	One of the chains forged by Thor to bind Fenrir, which broke.

Laeradr	A tree that is often identified with Yggdrasil. It stands at the top of Valhalla. Two animals, the goat Heidrun and the hart Eikthyrnir, graze on its foliage.
Mead of Poetry	A mythical beverage that whoever drinks becomes a skald or scholar to recite any information and solve any question.
Megingjord	A magic belt worn by Thor that doubles his strength. Translates as 'Power-belt'.
Mimameidr	A tree whose branches stretch over every land, unharmed by fire or metal, bearing fruit that assists pregnant women.
Mimir's Head	The decapitated head of Mimir, which was magically preserved by Odin so it could continue to provide knowledge and counsel as his advisor.
Mimisbrunnr	A well associated with Mimir, located beneath Yggdrasil. The water of the well contains much wisdom. Translated as 'Mimir's well'.
Mjolnir	A magical hammer wielded by Thor. It is invulnerable and when thrown returns to the user's hand.
Naglfar	A ship made out of fingernails and toenails of the dead. It will set sail during Ragnarok.
Odin's Eye	Odin sacrifice his eye to Mimir for the price of wisdom, a drink from the Mimisbrunnr.
Ódrerir	One of the vessels that contains the Mead of Poetry.
Ran's Net	A net in which Ran uses to capture men who ventured out on the sea.
Rati	A drill that was used by Odin during his quest to obtain the mead of poetry.
Ridill	A sword belonging to the dwarf Regin.
Sacred tree at Uppsala	A sacred tree at the Temple at Uppsala, Sweden, in the second half of the 11th century. Possibly a Yew tree.
Sessrumnir	Freyja's hall located in Folkvangr, a field where Freyja receives half of those who die in battle, and also the name of a ship.
Singasteinn	An object that appears in the account of Loki and Heimdallr's fight in the form of seals. Translates as 'singing-stone'.
Skidbladnir	A ship owned by Freyr. Described as the finest of ships.
Skofnung Stone	A stone that can heal wounds made by the sword Skofnung.
Skofnung Sword	Legendary sword of Danish king Hrolf Kraki. Supernaturally sharp and hard. A cut made by Skofnung will not heal. The only way to stop this is by touching the cut with the Skofnung stone.
Son	One of the vessels that contains the Mead of Poetry.
Surtalogi	The fire the giant Surtr will burn the world with. Translates as 'Surtr's fire'.

Svalinn	A shield which stands before the sun and protects Earth from burning. If the shield were to fall from its frontal position, the mountains and seas would burn up.
Tarnkappe	Sigurd's magical cloak that makes the wearer invisible.
Thjazi's Eyes	Odin took Thjazi's eyes and placed them in the night sky as stars.
Thor's Chariot	Driven across the sky by Thor and pulled by his two goats Tanngrisnir and Tanngnjostr.
Thunderstone	Arrowheads and axes that appear in farmer's plows, considered to have fallen from the sky, often thought to be thunderbolts.
Tyrfing	A magic sword made by the dwarves that would never miss a stroke, would never rust, and would cut through stone and iron as easily as through clothes. The dwarves cursed it so that it would kill a man every time it was used and that it would be the cause of three great evils.
Ullr's Bone	Ullr could traverse the sea on his magic bone.
Urdarbrunnr	A well that lies beneath Yggdrasil, associated with a trio of norns (Urdr, Verdandi, and Skuld). Translates as 'Well of Wyrd'.
Valknut	Hrungnir's head, heart, and shield were made of stone. His heart had a peculiar shape, it was triangular due to which both the Valknut and the Triquetra have been called Hrungnir's heart.
Vidarr's Shoes	Consisting of all the extra leather pieces that people have cut from their shoes, which gave Vidarr unparalleled foot protection.
Ymir's Body Parts	Odin, Vili, and Ve used Ymir's blood to make the ocean, his bones to make the hills, his brain to make the clouds, his eyebrows to make Midgard (Earth), his hair to make the trees, and his skull to make the dome of the sky.

www.ingramcontent.com/pod-product-compliance
Lightning Source LLC
Chambersburg PA
CBHW081201020426
42333CB00020B/2586